Taking Part

SINGULAR

LIVES

The Iowa Series

in North American

Autobiography

Albert E. Stone,

Series Editor

Taking Part

A TWENTIETH-CENTURY LIFE

Robert Josephy

FOREWORD BY ALBERT E. STONE

UNIVERSITY OF IOWA PRESS ⍦ IOWA CITY

University of Iowa Press,

Iowa City 52242

Copyright © 1993 by

the University of Iowa Press

Printed in the United States

of America

Design by Richard Hendel

Printed on acid-free paper

Library of Congress

Cataloging-in-Publication Data

Josephy, Robert, 1903–

    Taking part: a twentieth-century life / by

Robert Josephy; foreword by Albert E. Stone.

        p. cm.—(Singular lives)

    ISBN 0-87745-412-4 (cloth)

    1. Josephy, Robert, 1903– . 2. Book

designers—United States—Biography.

3. Book design—United States—History—

20th century. 4. Horticulturists—

Connecticut—Bethel (Town)—Biography.

5. Political activists—United States—

Biography. I. Title. II. Series.

Z116.A3J69   1993

741.6′4′092—dc20

[B]   92-44857

                                        CIP

97 96 95 94 93 C 5 4 3 2 1

CONTENTS

Foreword *by Albert E. Stone*

Although the author of *Taking Part: A Twentieth-Century Life* would never claim in advance a distinguished place in the annals of American autobiography, Robert Josephy has, in fact, created a significant example of an unusual kind of autobiography—a nonagenarian's narrative. True, he was only eighty-nine when this manuscript was turned in to the University of Iowa Press to become volume 7 in the Singular Lives series. Thus his book doesn't quite match the long view backward achieved by our culture's most famous very old man's memoir: *The Autobiography of W. E. B. Du Bois: A Soliloquy on Viewing My Life from the Last Decade of Its First Century*. Nor would Josephy anticipate anything like the fame or influence of America's greatest black intellectual. Yet his life-story displays, on a narrower stage of history, some of the same advantages of writing the self out of many decades' experience, as well as some perhaps inevitable blinders on the aged autobiographer's eyes.

The notable advantages of a lengthy historical perspective are readily seen in *Taking Part*. Nonetheless, the reader must wait until the final chapters to realize fully what Josephy believes these lasting benefits to be. His is a twentieth-century life-story as the successful search for roots. Not easily achieved by older Americans in this century of bewildering changes, this goal is in large part realized because Josephy follows a simple, timeless definition of "success" and "roots": "I wanted, as does everyone, to be comfortable in my environment, to find satisfaction in my work, to enjoy and respect my neighbors." The paradox in achieving this basic formula is that the rural apple-grower and citizen of Bethel, Connecticut, who proclaims interdependence as the final key to a meaningful life, is the same self who earlier—and repeatedly—declared independence from many of the social institutions commonly rooting one in white American society. A family background of privilege, the ancient verities of traditional Judaism, a college education, allegiance to mainstream political parties, occupational security as typographer in a major Madison Avenue publishing house, fidelity within a monogamous marriage—each of these props of a successful upper middle-class identity is rejected in favor of a personal freedom sometimes carried to radical lengths.

In fact, Robert Josephy decided quite early "to shape for myself . . . in design, in social relations, in government, in land-use, the sort of world I want to live in." He became a pioneer free-lance book designer in New York. The reproductions scattered through these pages attest to the mastery acquired and help justify the opinion of a critic who termed him "the single most important figure in American trade book design during the crucial decade 1930–40." His clean, straightforward, sensitive work attracted contracts from a growing circle of American (and some foreign) publishers, both elite and mass market, conservative and innovative, traditional and radical in politics. By this means Josephy came to know and work with a number of famous writers, artists, publishers, and critics. Indeed, were it not for Josephy's candid comments on and pithy characterizations of friends and acquaintances like Alfred Stieglitz, Carl Sandburg, Alexander Calder, Malcolm Cowley, Lewis Mumford, Lillian Hellman, Claire Booth Luce, Alfred Knopf, and Arthur Miller, one might accuse him of name-dropping. Though this would be unfair, it's true Josephy's litany of names—extending ultimately well beyond Broadway and Madison Avenue to include ordinary folk like his parents' Scots handyman Robert Richardson and farming neighbors in Bethel—is more inclusive than his selective characterizations. As is commonly the case with aging authors, Josephy remembers vividly certain episodes and individuals from the further past but often cannot bring a similar concreteness to later experiences and relationships. Of a roommate from his bachelor days, for example, he remarks that memory "leaves me with too few anecdotes to tell about our long, close friendship but with unlimited affection and intimacy to remember."

Rather than trying to reconstruct dramatic scenes and conversations or making a pattern of metaphors to suggest continuity and connectedness in experience and character, this amateur author prefers less "literary" ways of authentication and specification. Thus *Taking Part*, like some other old men's memoirs, is liberally sprinkled with aphorisms, generalizations, and frankly didactic statements. Nuggets of memory as wisdom communicate a sense of sameness as well as change in his characteristic ways of encountering the world. Speaking of the heady years of his membership in the Book and Magazine Guild and left-wing politics, he terms himself "a small bore traitor" to his class. Such ironic diffidence underscores the playful seriousness with which he's pursued a lifelong aim, "to make a dent in the brittle body of tradition."

Similarly, the numerous episodes in his long history as lover and husband are recalled with frank enthusiasm. "Monogamy and fidelity are not clearly written in my rule book," he calmly asserts. As with other social and professional relationships, amorous and domestic experiences and difficulties are recreated in a series of candid and succinct descriptions. "I have always enjoyed the company of women and have spent a great deal of time with them, probably more than the average man. I have worked with them in the labor and environment movements, in publishing, and in politics. I have also sought their companionship for pleasure, comfort, and intellectual stimulation. Sometimes my interest has been frivolous, but many of my longest and most rewarding friendships began as romantic episodes." Whether female readers will endorse this claim is a risk Josephy willingly runs. In his defense, it is true that times have changed; the behavior and language of a carefree twenties bachelor, dancing on the sidewalk outside Delmonico's and dallying with would-be flappers, are sure to strike some nineties readers as quaintly but unmistakably sexist. On the other hand, Josephy's "late enlightenment" should not be rejected, based as it seems to be on a genuine gift for continuing or restoring relationships with both women and men. In this talent for keeping ties alive Josephy reminds me of another autobiographer—again, one more famous than he. In *Blackberry Winter* Margaret Mead demonstrates a remarkable openness and tolerance in discussing her three divorced husbands. Josephy is at least as candid as the world-renowned anthropologist in acknowledging his shortcomings as a marriage partner. Yet his narrative also memorializes his second wife, Martha, and celebrates an enduring relationship even after separation. "Neither Martha nor I has at any time contemplated divorce. . . . Now, late in our lives, I feel closer to her than I ever have. This increased affection and mutual dependency have brought our children closer too, in spite of geographical separation." Similar affection also characterizes his memories of his dead first wife and a number of past lovers, as well as his male companions.

The challenge of a suitable ending to an old man's memoir is, I think, amply met in *Taking Part*. Wrapping up the past in the present; celebrating relationships and values which have lasted; making amends and defending choices; looking ahead to the coming century and its challenges for American society, agriculture, and the environment; facing loneliness, illness, and death with hope and good humor; giving thanks for a pretty waitress and a stiff drink of whiskey before dinner in a retirement home—these are all signs of an acceptable and accepted life and of a successful and singular life-story. As with W. E. B. Du Bois and Margaret Mead, Robert Josephy reminds me of the Civil War battlefield comment by a French-speaking chaplain in John DeForest's *Miss Ravenel's Conversion*. Of his dying colonel (also a lover of many women), the padre remarks, "Il a maintenu jusqu'au bout son personnage."

Taking Part

1 🍎 *A Sheltered Childhood*

I was born on July 11, 1903, in my mother's bed in the Long Island summer house of her father, David Spero. I am completing this memoir in 1992, just after my eighty-ninth birthday, approaching the end of a life spent designing books and printing, helping to organize a trade union, operating a large commercial fruit farm, and working to conserve natural resources. I have also been active in politics and public affairs, and all through my life I have written essays, speeches, and letters to the press on technology and aesthetics and in support of my ideas. All this has shown my taste for polemics, perhaps overindulged at times.

For many years the Speros were as close to me as my parents, really closer than my father. Their affection, the stability and freedom of their household, and the economic cushion they provided gave me a sense of security which has been valuable to me throughout my whole life. Proper families, influenced no doubt by the masculinity of Teddy Roosevelt, did little hugging and cuddling of boys in those days, but I was still made to feel that I was the most cherished of children.

My grandfather, David Spero, left his family home in Syracuse, New York, at fourteen to make his fortune in New York City. He was a bit like the heroes of Horatio Alger's very popular books but without the pious and humorless nobility that was always shown to be the Alger heroes' way to financial and romantic success. By the time I was born he had accumulated a modest fortune as an importer of ladies' hat trimmings, known in the trade as "flowers and feathers." This was a flourishing business at a time when ladies made their own choices of elaborate, sometimes excessive, decorations to mount on each new hat.

My maternal grandmother, Sarah Hyams (always called by the diminutive Sadie), was a city girl whose parents came from England under sail in 1839. Her father went to California in the 1849 gold rush; he returned with a single nugget which he wore in a ring for the rest of his life. He became a manufacturer in New York of uniforms for policemen and firemen.

Grandpa's summer place, a huge wooden house on four acres in Far Rockaway, was close to the ocean on the south shore of Long Island in New York City's Queens borough. In those days city leaders thought of territorial expansion as the way to wealth and power. New York had recently absorbed Brooklyn, Staten Island, and Queens into a great megalopolis, with new transportation for commuters and new educational opportunities for their children. Some of my aunts and uncles settled in Queens and commuted to their jobs in Manhattan. Having them for neighbors added to the stability of my world. One of my uncles, Charlie Brodek, was a special favorite of mine. He was a successful lawyer whom I perceived even at that age as more thoughtful and independent than my other relatives. My sister, Marian, was born three years after me, and my brother, Willard, called Billy, three years later, but I can remember little of them in those early years.

Grandpa's house was built for summer use only, a typical seashore house with a dozen gables and what seemed to me to be a mile of porches. Big enough for his children and their friends and for any future offspring, the house was staffed by a large crew of underpaid women who had recently come from Ireland. All the furniture was wicker, and the curtains always seemed to me to smell like elephants. Having the run of such a house was a great experience for a small boy.

Three years after it was built, Grandpa had the house moved another hundred feet back from the road because he thought it would look better that way. Our house and grounds were among the largest in the town, with gardens, stables, a tennis court, and wide lawns, and it became a playground for my cousins and friends. Grandpa was obsessed by dandelions thriving in his sandy lawn. A convert to the new fad of golf, he recruited dozens of small caddies to attack the vile plants when things were slow at the links.

An important feature of Rockaway summers was our daily carriage trip to the beach. We would go there fully dressed and change in a bathhouse of our own, which was well stocked with Social Tea biscuits. There were thousands of huge beach umbrellas announcing, "All cars transfer to Bloomingdale's," and celebrating both the city's network of nickel-a-ride streetcars and the rise of great department stores.

Once I rode my bike to the beach alone, which was against the rules. I found a live crab, something I knew my mother fancied, but when I brought it to her I was spanked. Was I being naive or disingenuous or crafty? I really didn't know.

Long Island was mostly rural, with highly productive vegetable farms and nurseries on fertile soils that the great glacier had left as it melted its way back from the sea about 18,000 years earlier. We went to some of those farms to buy produce, but it certainly never occurred to me that I myself might someday become a farmer. We went to the big county fair at Mineola, to the polo matches at Westbury, and, as soon as it was built, for a ride on the Motor Parkway. That was an express road built by some wealthy men for speeding-up trips to their North Shore estates. We spent five months of each year with the Speros and the rest of the year in New York City, but when I think of my childhood I remember most those months in Far Rockaway.

I remember my appendectomy at age eight, keeping me two full weeks in the hospital and two more in bed at home, with the name of my dread affliction kept carefully from my innocent ears. I remember the tremendous excitement when one of our horses broke a leg in the barn and the mild excitement of my first sexual experience, an exchange of views of genitalia enjoyed by boys and girls under the front porch. This was followed by discovery and suitable punishment.

My parents' social life seemed to be quite sedate; they took little part in any revolt against Victorian prudery. I did hear them whisper about witnessing the new uninhibited dances. One was described in a song all the children knew:

Everybody's doing it. Doing what? Turkey trot.
See that ragtime couple over there.
See them throw their shoulders in the air . . .

I can still remember the tune.

My grandfather Spero was an amiable, gregarious, and humorous round-faced man with a small mustache, unimpressive in
a day of luxuriant whiskers. His business success owed a lot to
his outgoing personality before the days when selling got to be a
science. In New York he liked to take me walking on Sunday
mornings, and he seemed to know half the people on the street.
He would say to me, "Everybody knows Dave Spero," and I believed him.

Above everything else he was devoted to his family, and so was
my plump grandmother. She was the perfect wife for a nineteenth-
century self-made man, affectionate and supportive but not force-
ful, managing her big household competently, responding with
good humor to whatever was said or done. One of the few definite
things I remember about her was a persistent campaign to get me
to share her enthusiasm for Charles Dickens. Grandpa went to
Europe every year to buy flowers and feathers. If my grandmother
did not go with him, he would bring back elaborate presents for
her and for my mother.

He was only fifty when he retired from his business. His formal
education had ended at fourteen, and his cultural resources were
limited; inactivity soon bored him. One of his few enthusiasms
was the theater, which he attended and supported faithfully. He
also took me to vaudeville shows on many a Saturday afternoon.
Religion meant nothing to him, but he was a great admirer of the
famous rabbi Stephen Wise, and I went with him now and then to
Wise's services, pragmatically held on Sundays at Carnegie Hall.
Grandpa said Wise would have made a great Shakespearean actor,
and many people agreed.

Like many businesspersons, he dabbled in real estate and became
the active manager of two loft buildings he owned, setting up his
office in one of them. He enjoyed himself enormously, quarreling
with his immigrant tenants. Most of them operated small sweat-
shops in the days before the Ladies' Garment Workers Union
brought economic order and economic justice to that industry.

I cannot say that Grandpa's natural goodwill and tolerance ex-

David Spero

tended to these new rough-diamond Americans struggling for a share of the dream that had brought them from European ghettos. Grandpa certainly did not come from a prosperous family, and he must have started life with few class prejudices. During thirty or forty years as a thriving owner and employer he acquired with his new status a standard set of bourgeois attitudes. This became a significant social lesson for me when I grew old enough to see and understand it.

Many of our friends in Far Rockaway were prosperous, entrenched families descended from mid-nineteenth-century German-Jewish immigrants. During the First World War some of them changed their names; the Minzesheimers became Mintons; the Berolzheimers, Berols; the Litchensteins, Lanes. How much of that was a concession to the strong anti-German feeling of the time and how much an opportunistic step to move closer to the American social and cultural mainstream was never clear.

Among our neighbors were the Samuel Knopfs, whose daughter Sophia was being courted by my uncle Alvin Josephy. My family did not admire Sam (neither did I when I knew him well years later), but that fortunately did not stop the couple from marrying after Alvin graduated from Cornell. It was indirectly through them that I ended up working for Sophie's brother Alfred.

In those days the automobile, conceived in the eighties and born a little before I was, was the tremendous new fact of life. My father owned a steam-powered Locomobile, and my mother was the first female in town to be seen driving. Autos were inclined to break down; public garages were scarce and mechanics lacked experience, so drivers had to make their own repairs. Grandpa sent Hugh Woolford, the family coachman, to an automobile school in Troy, New York, to study the mysteries of the new machines. Total acceptance of the modern miracle came when Hugh returned, full of new technical knowledge and skills. We got our first family car, and the horses were retired. Our stable became the garage, with gasoline stored in cans in a covered pit outside.

Most of the best early automobiles were built by hand in Europe, sometimes with only the chassis imported, to be fitted with a body by an American carriage builder. We had one of those, with separate bolt-on bodies for winter and summer. There was also a sporting car for the young people with no top, four bucket seats, a poncho-style cover for sudden storms with holes for four heads, and matching rubber hats for the passengers.

A sight-seeing trip by motorcar, called touring, was an annual rite for my grandparents and their friends. Most roads were unpaved, goggles and linen dusters a necessity. There were no road signs, and people traveled with guidebooks which showed every turn and landmark; a hundred miles was considered a good day's tour. There were frequent stops to repair tires; rubber was not very tough, and there were many stories of tacks and glass scattered on the roads to stop cars and bring customers to garages and inns.

Henry Ford introduced the assembly line to the automobile industry, and, as everyone knows, the industry developed quickly. Soon cheap American cars were being made by the millions, and by the time I was fifteen I was driving one of the famous Model T Fords. Drivers' licenses were required only of chauffeurs and truck drivers. I had a Ford of my own two years later, and for the rest of my life I was never without a car and occasionally a second one.

I began life in a sheltered, comfortable world into which the conflicts and stresses of existence could not penetrate, in which my happy family did not want them to be perceived. At first I naturally accepted the values and attitudes of that world and knew no other, but even before adolescence I began to question some of those values. I began to see how my family's prosperity had led to acceptance of the privileges of their class and to a kind of helplessness in the face of the simple mechanics of living. Later, under the influence of Marxist thought, I learned to call these traits bourgeois. Ironically, though, the sense of security I gained in the shelter of my family made it easier for me to oppose the ideas and actions of their world when I later became alienated from it.

I inherited a strong body and good looks from my parents, with my mother's fair hair and blue eyes. Combined with the strong sense of security I had from childhood, these physical attributes had no little effect on people's reaction to me, and not all of it was good. I learned at an early age that few people were indifferent to me. Wherever I went, whatever I did, I always drew the lightning, which was true throughout my life. To many I seemed arrogant and lacking in humility, while in others I inspired confidence.

When I was growing up I coined a motto for myself: "A new disillusion is better than an old one." Some people have called that cynical and negative. To me it has meant a positive commitment to keep seeking new challenges and experiences. It helped me to move easily into new ventures, each of which seemed to be the logical sequel to what I was doing. I never had a life plan, a neat matrix into which to fit my growth and my work. Most of my choices were made as needs and opportunities appeared, adding new proj-

Clarice Spero, about 1899

ects to old ones, bringing to my life variety, rewards, and some-times stress.

I cannot remember when I first realized that things inside my family were not as idyllic as they seemed. Although my mother, Clarice, and the Speros were the center of my childhood existence, my father, Edward, was by no means in the background. As I soon learned, he was a complex and unhappy man, outwardly aggressive but with many terrible weaknesses offset by some great strengths. The Speros never admired him. He was very different from them in temperament, and they must have feared that he would not be the sort of loving husband they wanted for their beloved daughter. I do not believe, however, that they ever tried to influence her; letting her have the man she loved was an expression of their affection.

My mother had been a famous blond beauty with many suitors. I once heard that her school friends the Morgan brothers, sons of an Irish family whose moving vans were seen all over New York, used to refer to her as "the Jewish Madonna." She was raised in an indulgent and not very sophisticated family, before there was any popular understanding of psychology to help young people look objectively at their peers and make realistic choices about their lives. She could not see that my father's impressive physical attractions and satisfactory family background were hardly enough basis for a marriage. Many years later she finally admitted her mistake to me and named a certain physician who had courted her as the man she should have married.

My other grandfather, Hugo Josephy (the emphasis is on the second syllable), was a rather stern Prussian gentleman. He was born in the tiny town of Ludwigslust, near Hamburg in northern Germany, where his family had been for several centuries. His ancestors were Sephardic Jews who had fled Portugal in the fifteenth century at the time of the Inquisition. Opportunities in Ludwigslust were limited, and in 1861 Hugo and his older brother Wilhelm sailed for New York, leaving their two sisters. Ships had no wireless in those days, and they were surprised to find when they landed that the Civil War had begun. How Hugo was first employed I do not know.

In his thirties he married seventeen-year-old Gertrude Klein from Bridgeport, Connecticut. When I knew him he had a business in New York wholesaling western-grown poultry and other produce, and my father was his partner. Hugo and Gertrude were powerful people, and we were always a little afraid of them. Hugo was austere and somewhat remote, with a wry and frequently sarcastic sense of humor; we thought him "strict." Gertrude was outgoing and energetic; people two generations later would have called her an executive type. Hugo died in 1915 at seventy-two after being hit by a streetcar, but Gertrude lived another thirty

An early nineteenth-century Josephy couple

years enjoying her position as matriarch at the center of family parties and crises. I remember her sister, Florence Bishop, childless and "musical," who came from Bridgeport to most of Grandma's parties, where we were required to applaud her sentimental singing and playing.

I also remember Hugo's brother, Uncle Billy, who came to America with him in 1861 and by coincidence ended up in the same line of business as my grandfather Spero. Uncle Billy was a lifelong bachelor, a sinful thing in the minds of good nineteenth-

century Jewish ladies. When he was old he lived in a small hotel apartment, cluttered with a huge collection of Napoleona (Billy was a very short man, like Napoleon). By the time I knew him his remaining pleasures were food and wine. He would drive out to lunch at country restaurants famous for their food, accompanied only by his valet and his dog, in a limousine equipped with plumbing to accommodate his wine-ruined kidneys. When he died, the art dealers, who had always exploited him shamelessly, bought his art collection at bargain prices. They left only a huge crystal chan-

Hugo Josephy, about 1902

delier which someone had to be paid to take away. No doubt the ladies were right in predicting that he would come to a bad end without a good woman to guide him.

My father was a complex and basically unhappy man. I can only guess at the early effect of his powerful parents on his character and personality. Their first-born, he joined his father in business at seventeen or eighteen and lived with them until he married at twenty-four. He was a handsome man, rather Latin in appearance, like his father. He loved horses, was a good rider, and strove all his life to be known as a horseman. He cared a great deal about his attire, but he made his good taste into an assertion of superiority. He had a veneer of self-confidence but little talent for relaxed relations with intimates or strangers. Like many insecure people, he was frequently aggressive in his manner and intolerant in his opinions.

As time went on, he found it harder and harder to accept everyone's preference and affection for my mother, and he was jealous of his children's easy relations with her. He had deep inhibitions about sexual matters. He could not bring himself to utter the word "sex" when, at the appropriate time, he tried to tell me the facts of life. One time at dinner he was asked what a capon was. It is a castrated rooster, but he could not manage to explain that in the presence of children and answered, "I'll tell you later." My parents' sexual life, however, was apparently satisfying. I remember when I was thirteen or fourteen hearing sounds in the house confirming this, even though at the time their conflicts about their children and about family finances were making my mother miserable.

He had a terrible secret: when he was about eighteen he had contracted syphilis. There was then no cure for the disease, but it was quiescent for many years, and he was able to conceive three healthy children in his twenties. No one knew his secret until he was nearly fifty, when serious neurological disorders were traced to his early infection. Having that experience as a youth, and concealing his secret for so many years, put pressures on him we knew nothing about. If we had known the story earlier, his behavior would have been easier to bear. By the time we did learn it, Clarice had been his wife for twenty-five years and his children were grown.

Although I remember most events of my childhood with great clarity, I find it hard to recall details of my father's behavior toward his wife and children. This contrasts so sharply with the fullness of my other recollections that I must conclude that I do not want to remember. My sister thinks that she too must have blocked out memory of his harsh and unreasonable efforts to establish the control which only uninhibited love and genuine tolerance could have gained for him.

Edward's father died in 1915, and without his strong hand the family business suffered, ties to old customers weakened, and friction between my father and Alvin, his younger brother and partner, increased. What did I learn from my father? He preached morality to us, but his brand of textbook virtue was not very convincing. His frequent inhumanity toward our mother, intolerance toward others, contempt for the less fortunate—these were things I could not admire. In sum, I have to say that my father's unwitting gift to me was a sharp perception of traits I did not want to make my own.

The people on both sides of my family were Jews, but they had little interest in Jewish customs and few vestiges of historic Jewish culture. They did make gestures of loyalty and adherence to their faith; they looked on converting to Christianity as vulgar and unthinkable. I never heard them talk about religion, and I don't believe they thought much about it. They took for granted their gradual integration into mainstream Anglo-Saxon Protestant culture, while still maintaining links to the Jewish community and label. They practically never went to synagogue; I never went to Hebrew school; there was no pressure of any kind on me to accept Jewish doctrine or to observe Jewish customs.

Like most Jews, my family used words taken from ancient Yiddish literature. The same words were used in Germany when my grandfather was growing up there. They were borrowed from secular speech and books and had no special religious significance. Many of these words, like "chutzpah," "schlemiel," and "nebbish," eventually became part of the American vocabulary.

My mother was a good friend of Rabbi Stephen Wise. She worked with him in various public welfare enterprises but took no part in religious observances. Spiritual enrichment was not offered me; philosophically I was always on my own. My chief contact with organized religion was during my four years at boarding school, and although I tried a variety of Protestant samples there, I never did buy. I did become acquainted with the Bible and have always been grateful for that. I don't think I was ever asked directly whether I believed in a supernatural deity. I would have had to say that I did not, so I guess I qualified early as an atheist, as I understand the meaning of the term.

As I try, late in life, to understand my early indifference to religion, I can see that I reacted instinctively against the hypocrisies I saw, against the failure of people who pretended to hold religious principles, to be guided by them in their daily lives. I know, too, that I very much wanted to construct a world for myself according to my own ideas, to make my own rules and set my own limits. No doubt it was arrogant to think I could do this without a God. I have of course paid some price for that, and I may be judged for it in the end, but by whom I cannot imagine.

I have no feeling of superiority to believers, and sometimes I envy them the comfort they find in faith and ritual. I used to be puzzled by scientist friends' ability to spend six days in the laboratory and one in church. In time, I learned from them how an internal spiritual life can be lived without accepting, but still without openly rejecting, the dogmas of organized religion. I cannot bridge in my own mind, however, the gap between science and religion.

Despite these reservations, I have always retained a sense of my ethnic if not my religious identity with Jews. I have always had a strong curiosity as to who was Jewish and who was not. I can't help but think that Jews should be expected to behave better than other people, so I am unreasonably outraged by the doings of Jewish crooks on Wall Street and in politics and contemptuous of the efforts of nouveau riche Jews to climb into the vulgar circles of newspaper "society." The recent movement of one-time Jewish radicals (some of whom I once knew) into conspicuous positions as the intellectual leaders of the political right-wing seems to me very little different from the social climbing of their bourgeois cousins.

I was proud of the success of the Jews when they established an independent democratic nation and made it strong and prosperous. I was not so proud later of their treatment of the Palestinians. I knew that the existence of Israel was endangered, but somehow I thought that their superior moral character should have enabled them to act with more generosity and magnanimity.

I have encountered anti-Semitism, of course. When I was still dating schoolgirls I found that some of their parents did not approve of their going out with me, but as I grew older my interests threw me among people to whom religion, whether their own or anyone else's, was of little importance. Looking back, I have to say that being born a Jew had very little influence on my life.

I do recall one painful incident in the late fifties. I was part of the top leadership of the New York and New England Apple Institute, the growers' sales promotion agency. When I was clearly in line to be the next president, I was suddenly maneuvered out of the nomination. It was done by John Chandler, head of an old entrenched Massachusetts farm family, who called all the shots in Institute affairs. John had always been most friendly, and I was puzzled until I recalled that he had used the term "kike" in speaking of Henry Morgenthau, Jr., a gentleman farmer friend of Franklin Roosevelt and his treasury secretary. End of puzzlement.

When I was young, I did see a lot of anti-Semitism *among* Jews. Those of western European origin, born and educated in America, felt threatened by a new wave of poor Jews from eastern Europe. I first heard the word "kike" when my own family used it to describe the tenants in Grandpa's loft buildings and to describe other recent immigrants who were rising rapidly in business and social circles. Jews were of course not entirely comfortable with this kind of prejudice; there was an often-heard joke, "a kike is any Jew but yourself," but the prejudice survived many years of social change. By World War II, however, this division among Jews had largely disappeared. The Nazis put an end to whatever remained of it.

2 🍎 *An Education of Sorts*

For a dozen years, from May through September, we lived with the Speros on Long Island. These months are the most memorable part of my childhood. The experiences that went with summer outdoor freedom were more important to me than my seven months of city life. Relations with my father, difficult for all of us, were also easier to bear in the Speros' large house than in the close quarters where we spent winters.

In New York City my parents had a small apartment, first on West 88th Street and then on 94th Street near Riverside Drive, from which we could glimpse the Hudson River. One of my earliest memories is seeing the Hudson-Fulton centennial celebration, with dozens of warships sailing up the river and President William Taft triumphant on the deck of one of them. I rode on the 86th Street crosstown horsecar, one of the last to be electrified, and I watched for the lamplighter coming to ignite the gas street lamps at twilight. I remember a bloody carriage ride home from having my tonsils removed and a bitter battle with my mother to let me have my blond curls cut off. My first public entertainment was "Little Nemo," a big musical show based on a favorite comic strip character.

About 1908 my father bought a brownstone house on 77th Street near Riverside Drive. New York had thousands of these nineteenth-century houses. Mostly twenty feet wide, they were separated by brick walls which supported the wood floor joists and were faced with red-brown sandstone. The bricks came from clay deposits along the upper Hudson River and much of the stone from a quarry on the Connecticut River at Portland; both materials were barged to the city on the rivers and on Long Island Sound. In winter a bitter west wind blew off the Hudson and up our street.

At this time young middle-class families were moving from east of Central Park to the west side. I played with neighborhood children in Riverside Park and spent rainy days in the immense and fascinating American Museum of Natural History a few blocks from our house. I started kindergarten at Public School 9 on West End Avenue. It was not a big building, and after the third grade the boys were required to transfer to a school further east on Amsterdam Avenue. The children there were said to be less polite than those at P.S. 9 and perhaps not as well washed. To protect me from the horrors of associating with them I was sent at age nine to the Hamilton Institute for Boys, a private school.

Hamilton Institute provided my first real encounter with my family's strong commitment to middle-class social values, to their sense of being different from those they called working-class people. Two years later I had a second such experience. We were giving up our big summer house in Far Rockaway. Jewish families we called "undesirable" were invading our territory, and we fled to escape them, as "respectable," entrenched people have always done. What made these new neighbors undesirable? Their recent arrival from eastern Europe, their different manners and customs, and their financial success seemed to threaten our own position. Grandpa sold his dream house to one of them.

Does that mean that my family was unfriendly, filled with prejudices and insecurities? I do not remember it that way. Prosperity brought with it convictions of social and cultural superiority. We hated nobody, but we believed that people on lower economic or cultural levels were somehow less sensitive, bled less when cut, shivered less when cold, valued less the blessings of civilization. These beliefs kept us comfortably free of any feeling of guilt for our privileged position. It was, of course, natural for us to extend this attitude toward newcomer neighbors, however prosperous.

For two summers we rented a house near Long Island Sound in

At age two, 1905

Great Neck, a house smaller than the big one in Rockaway. I over-heard some talk that Grandpa's income was shrinking, but I cannot estimate how much the move was due to snobbery and how much to economy. For me, Great Neck was a fine place. I was eleven and could have a rowboat on the Sound; I could go fishing and trap eels in eelpots. Evenings we could meet the steamboat bringing commuters home from the city and could help tie it to the wharf. My mother loved the water; she and I spent many days fishing from our flat-bottom rowboat.

I went to Hamilton Institute for a year. It was a long walk to school, there were many fascinating construction projects along the way, and I was late to school regularly. Then, before the year was out, I made an enemy of my teacher. One day when I was "kept in" he was entertaining a young female instructor in the next room, and I decided to make him pay for punishing me. I made loud suggestive noises reflecting on the purity of his interest in the lady. He rushed in and pelted me with blackboard erasers. Later, his father, who happened to be the headmaster, advised sending me to a school with more discipline. My family took this very seriously; they knew well what a bad character I could be, and at ten I ended up at an elementary-grade military school in Freehold, New Jersey. Somehow, sometime, I skipped a year, and I started my two years there in the sixth grade.

Major Duncan, the head of the school, was a high-church-with-incense Episcopalian, and we were all required to go to services. He also believed in traditional teaching, so Latin was one of our regular studies.

There were many military schools in those days. The country was enjoying its newly won imperial power, and militarism was looked on as a synonym for discipline and thought to be an excellent foundation for a good education. There was actually very little that was really martial about Freehold. We wore uniforms, Spanish-American War style, and we drilled with older cadets from a school across town, but we were allowed to be children. I don't recall that being away from home distressed me at all.

Freehold was a pleasant, quiet town, the center of what was then one of the most fertile New Jersey farm areas. There was a big Monmouth County fair each fall, with trotting races, and we knew where to find holes under the fences.

I must have developed a strong curiosity about the female body at that early age; I was caught peeking at a teacher's wife in her bath. I spent a week or two in terror of the consequences, but there were none, except for a milder and more understanding lecture than I expected. I don't know how I got this special curi-

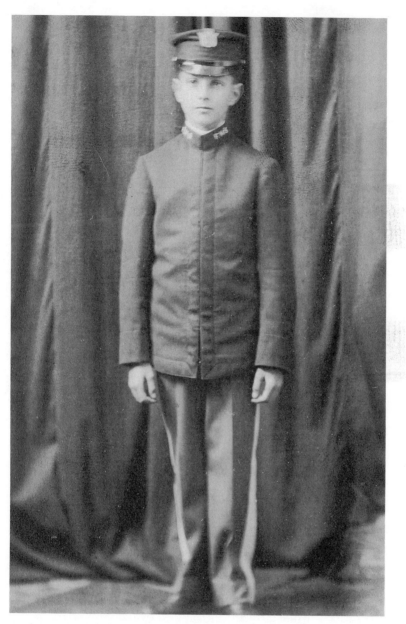

At Freehold, *1913*

osity. Perhaps it was due to the then current practice of Victorian prudery; the women at the beach were covered from head to toe with bathing dresses and stockings. I can still remember noticing the bodies of certain girls at school blooming at twelve or thirteen. As an adult, privileged to enjoy plenty of intimacies, I still find myself staring at waitresses, sometimes to the annoyance of my companions.

The First World War began in Europe in 1914 while I was still away at Freehold. Although the United States did not declare war until 1917, anti-German sentiment developed early, much of it stimulated by propaganda stories of atrocities in Belgium. There was a strong German cultural tilt in my family, coming from our German origins. I came home for my 1915 summer vacation to find that my sister's German governess had been replaced by an English lady. We were naturally uneasy about my grandfather Hugo's German roots, but I do not recall any unpleasant incidents related to that.

We were at war during most of my remaining time at school. As I remember it, the American people were not deeply involved emotionally, except, of course, those who had relatives in France, bogged down in the endless, senseless, trench warfare. No one from my family was in the service, but we did our small share. In 1915 or 1916 in Flushing, we plowed our yard and grew potatoes, and I developed a few other war enterprises. There was always substantial support, some of it well organized and vocal, for the idea that we should not have taken any part in the war at all. Certainly few people believed, as they did in another war a generation later, that the survival of civilization was at stake and that full emotional and physical commitment should be asked of everyone.

After I had been at Freehold for two years my family rented out their Manhattan brownstone and went to live in Flushing, on Long Island. I knew that this was an economy move. Why it was necessary I was not told, but it was the first of several moves to save money and still keep up appearances. Our house there, large and old, had been the center of an estate, but modest suburban dwellings had been built on all the land, and the big house was a sort of white elephant surrounded by them.

Flushing was a historic town with good soil and fine trees, known for its excellent nurseries and truck farms. A twenty-minute railroad trip from Manhattan, it was losing its small-town character but was still rural enough to make life pleasant for an adolescent boy. I joined a Boy Scout troop, and I went bird-watching with my friends the Donaldson brothers, who were devoted to that pursuit though sometimes optimistic in their identifications of species.

Flushing, 1915

We had a tree in the yard big enough for a tree house. There were woods nearby, and Long Island Sound was only a bicycle ride away.

Our family plan for an economical life-style still permitted us to have a man and woman to do housework and general maintenance.

This was not the custom in our neighborhood and was sometimes an embarrassment. I remember being driven to high school on a rainy day and getting out of the car around the corner to avoid the shame of being caught with what my friends would think was a chauffeur.

This man, Robert Richardson, was a Scotsman who became my close companion. An accomplished jack-of-all-trades, he taught me about tools and materials, and we had a good workshop in the basement. I developed a thriving trade in birdhouses and knitting stands, the latter a device to increase the efficiency of women making socks and sweaters for soldiers. Robert was chiefly responsible for my becoming a practical carpenter, metalworker, mason, and electrician, all useful skills to have later when I had a house and a farm to take care of and no money.

While I was still in school I began to accumulate hand tools of my own. Much later, when I had on my farm a small building to use for a shop, I added power tools and could make and repair equipment, make store fixtures, and build furniture. The rewards of working with wood are well known; to use lumber from one's own trees, as I sometimes did, doubles the pleasure.

I do not remember my mother doing any gardening in Far Rockaway. She may have been too young and too absorbed in her three small children, and she may have been discouraged by the professional gardeners there. In Flushing she began to learn how to care for flowers and shrubs and then to grow some vegetables. Close as I always was to her, this must have sowed seeds in me that germinated many years later.

Flushing had a daily paper, the *Evening Journal*, and at fourteen I joined the staff as a fifteen-cents-per-column-inch writer and general office nuisance. The reporters called me Brisbane, the name of a famous Hearst journalist, and used me for ancient newspaper office gags such as sending me to hunt for a paper stretcher. Each month I pasted my stories onto a long sheet so they could be measured for my pay. They were mostly about school doings, but once the paper printed my piece about the death of the butcher Sleuter's horse. I did have the run of the plant and could watch the compositors, the linotypers, and the pressmen. I found this to be useful knowledge a few years later when I was working on the production of books. This acquaintance with the mechanical side of publishing may be what led to my having a career as a designer rather than as a writer.

Sometime in my thirteenth year my childhood ended. My neighbor, Medora Weymouth, running to her aunt's house near our school, changed before my eyes from just a person to a female. Suddenly I entered what for the rest of my life would be a divided world. I continued for a while to sing soprano with the girls at school, but things were changing. The sudden obligation to uphold all the responsibilities of the male sex must have frightened me. My feelings developed faster than my courage. I dodged doing my duty in spin-the-bottle kissing games, even in the darkened room to which one retired with the lucky partner. At thirteen Marjorie Taylor and I were in love, but I never kissed her.

I certainly became aware of how girls were made. I remember a glimpse of Medora's bare knee when we sat on her lawn. Walking to school behind some neighbors, I observed that one of Mildred O'Connell's calves was not as sturdy as the other, and Jo Fitzpatrick already had the overdeveloped legs and hips that distress many grown women. I saw that Jo Kerwin's breasts bounced when she ran.

At high school a few girls were already stirring fantasies and gossip. There was Marjorie Page, only a freshman but so pretty and aware of her powers that she was being rushed by all the older boys. And there was a girl who lived in the Corona slums, literally the other side of the track, who was widely believed to be available for real sex.

Marjorie Taylor gave me up because I didn't write to her even once while I was at summer camp. The next year I fell in love with Clarissa De Willers, who seemed always to be in sight in class and in the halls. I never spoke to her, but I knew she loved me, too. Fifteen years later I was told that she worked for a publisher and had asked about me. Did I go see her then? I did not, though I could never figure out why. I can see now that those intense feelings about girls hit me years before I knew how to act on them.

When I was fourteen I had the tremendous social experience of graduating from knickerbockers to long trousers, a landmark rite. That year I was introduced to the pleasant and sometimes comforting practice of masturbation, of which I had never even heard. My father gave me one of the pamphlets, common in those days, warning boys of moral and physical degradation usually ending in insanity. Naturally I investigated promptly.

We had a neighborhood movie theater operated by the owner and a projectionist and otherwise staffed by us unpaid schoolboys. I saw the best shows of the silent film days there. Downtown we could see genuine sex: Mack Sennett's bathing beauty films. This was an enlightening experience; the girls we knew wore stockings when swimming, and only the boldest rolled theirs below the knee.

Summers my family managed to get away from Flushing for a while. Twice we had cottages in northwest Connecticut. My sharpest memories of those days are of wrestling huge blocks of ice out of a hot, airless icehouse for my mother and the neighbors and battling a primitive and stubborn outboard motor when I went fishing. I also went to a boys' camp in Maine and another year to a hotel in the Adirondacks where I was induced to try golf. That was a great mistake; I was addicted to the game for six or seven years. I became fairly good at it, but the notorious frustrations, the costs, and the boring company at the golf club finally drove me to quit. I have never regretted the decision.

I lived in Flushing for three years, where I attended the eighth grade and Flushing High School. These schools were part of the immense New York public school system. As is still the case today, classes were too large and discipline was weak. Sometimes a group of two or three dozen boys would gather on a pleasant morning and decide to skip school. At the opening hour we would parade noisily past the more dutiful or timid students watching enviously from the windows and march several miles to the beach at Malba. With all my extracurricular interests, I was easily persuaded not to spend much time studying, and my marks showed it.

By the end of my second year at Flushing High I was approaching fifteen. The balance of power in the struggle with my father had shifted. I was no longer the little boy he could try to dominate, and my mother paid for his frustration. His nagging criticisms increased as our personalities developed. There was no corporal punishment for failing to meet his standards, but he was unable to show any affection when we were good. He believed that he was somehow superior to our neighbors and derided my mother's friendly relations with them. Her only support and comfort came from her close friend Margaret Rockwell, who was similarly trapped in an unhappy marriage.

My poor performance in public school was excuse enough for sending me away again, and the frictions within the family did not have to be openly acknowledged. It was said that since I had done well at Freehold, another military school seemed prescribed, so I was enrolled at the Bordentown Military Institute in New Jersey.

Bordentown was an old institution which Colonel Thomas D. Landon, U.S. Army Retired, had inherited from his father, a Methodist preacher. An authentic Colonel Blimp type, Colonel Landon was pompous and unimaginative. He had no rapport with the students and dealt with their problems without flexibility or compassion. Fortunately, an older cousin inherited the school along with the colonel. Sealand Whitney Landon, an austere solemn man but a serious educator, established a rigorous curriculum and an excellent faculty. He died during my first year at BMI, but his standards survived several mediocre successors.

The school buildings were old. The huge original structure contained a meeting hall, classrooms, dormitories, and an attached gymnasium. Several adjoining residences had been annexed for housing cadets.

Bordentown lay south of Trenton on the Delaware River. There were deposits of good clay there, and the town was built all of brick; even the streets were paved with it. On Sunday afternoons, our only time at liberty, we walked to the brickworks, to Molly Pitcher's Well where a heroine of the American Revolution had ministered to the troops, and to the abandoned estate of a genuine Bonaparte which had a secret escape tunnel to the riverbank.

For me the change could not have been sharper. After three years of small-town freedom in Flushing with many opportunities and diversions, I suddenly found myself in the rigid structure of a military academy, its routines copied from West Point and other institutions for training armed service professionals. Most of our time was tightly scheduled. There was a complicated system of privileges and punishments; advance in military rank was the prime objective.

We had little contact with females. Glee club performances were exchanged with one girls' school, and we also shared an annual military drill with the uniformed young women of Ogontz Academy. We had a few tightly chaperoned dances with formal dance cards. A responsible senior boy could invite a Bordentown girl to the monthly cultural evening and escort her home. If he was bold enough and quick about it he might accomplish a good-night kiss.

The teaching was well above the notoriously low level of most military schools. The teachers were all civilians. Though we were required to salute them on campus, they returned our salutes with embarrassed distaste. The evening study hall was an important part of the system. The entire cadet corps gathered in one large room. The unfortunate teacher in charge that week had to patrol the aisles constantly to spot boys whispering, reading forbidden literature, or simply daydreaming. A few of us with good grades were rewarded by a place on the weekly "upstairs list," which allowed us to study in our rooms.

This carrot-and-stick practice kept me at my books. I absorbed a lot of information in two years and found a new pleasure in learning. I doubled up in French, taking two years in one, scored 100 percent on a College Board geometry test, and had other academic triumphs. I also edited and wrote a large part of the school magazine. Later I received an extra, unexpected dividend from my good academic performance: it gave me a measure of immunity when my rebellion against the establishment got me into trouble.

My two years at BMI, at the sensitive age of fifteen and sixteen, was a time of intense self-awareness and exercise in self-improvement. I felt I needed lessons in physical courage so, although younger and lighter than many others, forced myself to play football with the scrubs. This cost me a great effort; I was really never good at contact sports, though I had always been a strong swimmer and a good shot.

One day I took part in one of the landmark fistfights in BMI history. My roommate and I, arguing with two other boys about some trivial matter, challenged them to battle. Fights between cadets were thought to be good growing experiences and were tolerated, even encouraged, by the faculty. My opponent, Elston Wickham, and I went to the gymnasium with a large audience of boys and a few teachers. We traded blows for over half an hour. We were quite evenly matched, but in the end I managed to outlast my foe. The other two boys decided not to fight. Wickham and I later became good friends.

I felt myself too self-conscious before my peers, so I decided to specialize in what was called elocution: reciting, with appropriate feeling, other people's florid prose and poetry. I had some success at this. I became a nonmusical feature on programs of the glee club and also declaimed regularly at academic ceremonies. One oration which I wrote myself was on religion as a permanent institution. Without any research I assumed that since most people had worshipped some sort of deity, there had to be a supernatural power. This schoolboy conviction did not long survive my later exposure to the outside world. Hard as I tried, however, I never overcame my self-consciousness on the platform until I was older and had something of my own to talk about.

At Bordentown we did not have much free time, but in the cellar of my dormitory house I managed to reconstruct an old armchair rescued from a trash pile. It became an unorthodox but tolerated feature of my Spartan living quarters and perhaps even encouraged study when I was on the "upstairs list."

We were always under pressure to conform, to be on time for every call with uniform in order, leather puttees polished, rifle handled smartly, mind fixed on promotion to a higher rank. Lack of precision at drill, lapses in dormitory neatness, talking and other misbehavior in class, failure to salute superiors, and an endless list of other offenses, large and small, brought penalties. The penalties were assignments to extra guard duty, aimless marching back and forth on the parade ground, guarding nothing. Worst of all, these penalties could be assessed by a cadet superior; if you were a private, even your corporal could punish you. The negative effect of this on the boys can be imagined—giving one boy this power over others could only produce intolerance, vengefulness, and a false righteousness. The difference between good boys and bad boys became exaggerated. I soon found it impossible to respect the virtues and values that such a system was intended to support.

At first I was a model cadet. With some experience at Freehold to start me off, I made quick progress at drill. I had been on the rifle team at Flushing High, and that also helped. Early in my second year I rose to the rank of acting color sergeant, but by that time I had become scornful of the establishment and its rules. I committed a string of offenses, some deliberate, some from indifference. The cadet officer-of-the-day kept the record of cadets' penalties, the hours of extra tour duty they owed. One day I had access to the record sheet and changed the number after my name. I did not hesitate; I was in a war; it was me against them—and I was caught.

I was called before a faculty meeting, reduced to the rank of private, and otherwise punished and branded. It was clear that the authorities did not know what to make of me. They were baffled by this boy who did so well in his classes and other activities but who still refused to fit into the school picture. The colonel was so frustrated that he even remarked at my "trial" that certain other cadets recently in trouble were also Jewish and that this might explain our bad behavior. (I should add that this was the only sign of religious prejudice, either by students or faculty, that I ever encountered at BMI.)

Bucking the establishment did not, however, make me popular among the cadets; most of them seemed satisfied with the system. There were three clubs with Greek letter names. Two of them had closed recreation rooms for their members' use, but I was not invited to join either of those. The third had no meeting room and much less prestige; I became president of that club. I wondered whether the commandant was able to blackball candidates, but such questioning did not spare me from an uneasy feeling that people did not like me. Fortunately, this lasted only until I learned how relations in the adult world differed from the artificial society at BMI.

Of course the war was going on, and military schools were all designated as part of the Reserve Officers Training Corps. We had an officer from the War Department assigned to us, a Major Mackenzie, who was obviously too slow-witted to command troops at the front. The major did not admire my attitude. When I graduated from BMI I received my official discharge from Washington, signed by him. His recommendation was: "Could serve as a corporal in time of emergency." I presume that is still my rating in the files of the Pentagon. The war ended before I graduated. My disillusion with militarism as I saw it at BMI apparently did not affect my patriotism, as I was still disappointed at not being old enough to enlist.

Before I left BMI I had regained a little standing with the authorities. As one of the commencement orators, I read an essay I had written on the high cost of living. What I took with me when I graduated, along with a substantial amount of information and experience, was the conviction that I could never live with the principles on which such institutions were based. My parents had sent me there because they thought I would benefit from the discipline. At Bordentown they thought they were teaching discipline; what they really taught was conformity. They used the rules and system of military discipline to force conformity to their ideas.

I have never resisted discipline and have seldom been irked by it. I have gladly accepted the discipline needed to follow the procedures of the printing trade and the strict requirements which nature imposes on one who would grow farm crops successfully. At BMI I learned the difference between discipline and conformity; it was one of my earliest and most valuable lessons.

I left Bordentown in June of 1920, happy to escape. I returned once for a class reunion, then never heard from the school again for nearly fifty years, when they sent me an appeal to support a project for building a new campus outside the town. I decided that I ought to check out my old attitudes, so I went to visit. Time had diluted some of the smug militarism of the early days, and the color of the cadet corps had changed. There were many black children in Bordentown but none at the school in my day. The school had always offered athletic scholarships, and now, after fifty years, the boys on scholarship were mostly black. They not only led in sports but had gained the ranking posts in the cadet hierarchy.

This new blood did not save the school, however. The new campus was never built, and in a few years BMI was gone. Across the country today a few military schools still survive, some of them now coed. There were about 160 such schools in the fifties but less than 30 by the end of the eighties. Two exhausting world wars fought with twentieth-century weapons took most of the glamour out of military life.

3 ♥ *Five Years with Knopf*

After I left Bordentown I spent the summer with my family at a large hotel in the White Mountains of New Hampshire. I funded some of my amusements there by conducting a part-time day camp for my brother and other small boys. Having turned seventeen, I also attacked earnestly the problem of learning about girls. Our financial situation had improved somewhat, and my family had moved from Flushing to a house in the Hartsdale section of Scarsdale, in Westchester County. I knew my mother welcomed this move; she had many friends in Westchester.

I had made up my mind that my years at BMI would be the end of my formal education. Princeton was near Bordentown, and for a time I had thought of studying there, but as I watched my friends in college I was not impressed by what they were learning. I did not have many serious friends in those days. Most of them looked on college as a place to meet people who might help their later business careers, and that is how my family saw it, too. I wanted no more of established institutions, whatever their standing and reputation. I wanted independence, and a job seemed the way to achieve it. At various times I took evening courses at Columbia University and at the New School for Social Research, but in 1920 I was anxious to get to work.

My first intention was to become a writer. I planned to look for a newspaper job, encouraged by my experience on school publications and the *Flushing Journal*. It happened, however, that my distant relative, Alfred Knopf, had a book publishing business five years old and growing fast. I had never met him, but I went to see him. I found him full of idealism; he told me that the returns from publishing were not material but intellectual, almost spiritual. That was heady stuff for his seventeen-year-old visitor, and I went to work in his office on September 20, 1920, for eight dollars a week.

As I soon found out, a job in a publishing office was not the best route to becoming a writer; in fact, I learned that the author and the publisher were not always friends. They were often at odds on business matters, such as royalties and money spent on advertising and sometimes on the author's right to free expression when that jeopardized profits.

It was exciting to have a job, however, and a writing career could wait. I was a glorified office boy on a staff of only eight. When our new novel, Floyd Dell's *Moon-Calf*, got glowing reviews, I had the thrill of opening the bookstore orders which flooded the office. I substituted for our single shipping clerk who was out sick during the World Series. I helped cope with a crisis caused by women in the book bindery who were cutting out for their friends juicy pages from a nineteenth-century French novel describing a love scene with details rarely printed in those days. I lived through the furor caused by Knopf's charging $2.50 for the first novel ever priced above $2.00, an experiment first condemned and then imitated by other publishers.

The women who worked at Knopf's had customs different from those I had known. There was a pretty blond named Olga Jicha. I asked for a date, and next day I was told that her boyfriend wanted to talk to me. I did not meet him, but I got the point. I admired an amateur actress in Millay's *Aria da Capo* and became acquainted with her on the commuting train. I found her quite sophisticated. I took her to dinner at a Broadway place more expensive than I expected, and the check took all my money except a dime. I was too embarrassed to ask my date for help, and we escaped past a gauntlet of muttering waiters. Next day I went back and paid the tip.

The girls in Scarsdale, where I lived with my family, were more my speed. There was a clique of high school girls called the Green Acres gang, all very beautiful. I made a special friend of Dorothy

Smart, who was born to the camera and became one of the first celebrated photographer's models. Her parents were feuding, and we often took Mrs. Smart to the movies with us.

Franklin Spier was in charge of both advertising and book production at Knopf's, and I was soon assigned to work with him. By the time I was nineteen his job had grown too big for one person; he became advertising and publicity manager, and I was given the job of producing the books. My assistant for a while was a young poet named Clifton Fadiman, but he was unhappy in a business office and became a book reviewer and then the chief judge at the Book of the Month Club.

I was responsible for typesetting, printing, and binding schedules; for handling proofs; for the reproduction of illustrations, when there were any; for commissioning binding designs and sometimes jacket designs; and for buying paper and other materials. It turned out that what talents I had were adapted to this work. I had always been fascinated by construction projects of all kinds and had some acquaintance with the printing process from my *Flushing Journal* days. Also I was quick at arithmetic, an indispensable skill before the computer age. In a year or two we were publishing a hundred titles a year and I was earning sixty dollars every week, pretty good pay for anyone in 1923.

Alfred Knopf was a unique figure in the publishing business. He made himself conspicuous in a field dominated by quiet, self-effacing men who shunned personal publicity. His advertisements were personally signed statements, and his taste in design made his books look different from others. Even his bright-colored haberdashery set him apart.

No doubt these traits got Alfred attention, but he was really a serious man and published many books that he knew could not pay their way. With most recognized American writers committed to other publishers, he found and brought to this country successful European authors not known here, such as Knut Hamsun, Sigrid Undset, and Henryk Sienkiewicz. Gradually he established, by the quality of his lists, a reputation that also brought to his imprint some of the best and best-selling American and British writers. The wide respect he eventually earned from fellow publishers came from his literary judgment and his innovative search for authors, and came in spite of his promotion of the Knopf name and personality.

Alfred had tremendous personal enthusiasm for each of his authors. Those who were also his special friends included Joseph Hergesheimer, the only man who could outshine Alfred sartorially, Carl Van Vechten, Floyd Dell, and of course H. L. Mencken and George Jean Nathan. Others frequently in our office were hardly literary stars but were quite salable commodities. One was Kahlil Gibran, an Arabian mystic poet and to my mind a colossal fake. Another was John V. A. Weaver, whose thin verses, "In American," met many people's need for a contemporary voice. Willa Cather was important to our house but was rather reclusive. I went to her Greenwich Village apartment once to work with her on proofs.

Alfred called on booksellers, as did many smaller publishers, and was able to turn his enthusiasm into sales even when critics did not agree with his praise. He was hardly a diplomat, but he made arrogance and insensitivity into a sort of asset. There was a widely told story about his visiting a struggling bookseller and asking him, "Do you call this a bookstore?"

Seeing him daily, I learned that his sense of mission sometimes led him to trade on his own ideals, whether cynically or not I could not tell. One time he was planning a collected edition of the works of Stephen Crane, the vigorous nineteenth-century author of *The Red Badge of Courage* and *Maggie: A Girl of the Streets*, whom the public was forgetting. Alfred thought he should be better known to average readers, but he chose to issue the books in a delicately designed, lavender-bound limited edition. To justify a high price, he asked his best-known authors to contribute forewords, thus making each volume a collector's item and ensuring its sale. I saw a letter to one of those authors, offering a pittance for the foreword and saying, "If I can make no profit on this venture, I will at least be performing a service to literature."

I grew less than fond of Alfred's wife, Blanche, who was his chief editor and who stayed with the company long after their personal ties cooled. Blanche had charm, good looks, and certainly some talent. How much her judgment of books came from Alfred I never knew. Clearly she complemented Alfred's difficulty in relating personally to some of their authors, but she had few smiles for people who could not advance her interests.

Two or three years after I started work with Knopf the house began growing rapidly. Alfred's father, Samuel—finally convinced that Alfred was not just a visionary—became active in the management of the business. Aggressive and insensitive, he displayed little consideration for people's feelings. I began to understand how Alfred's social unease and his drive to impress his personality on the publishing world could have come from his childhood under Sam's domination.

As for me, the more I learned about type and printing, the more I became interested in typographic design. As my taste developed I found it was quite different from Alfred's. He cared a great deal about how his books were made and had a deserved reputation for spending more than most publishers on style and materials, but I began to think that the books I was producing for him were too flamboyant. Often their style did not reflect their content. I saw that if I were to stay with him there would be clashes. I also became critical of his relations with employees and resentful of the intrusions of his hard-driving father.

By 1925 I could see that Alfred did not intend to allow any employee to become too important to his business. I had an assistant, Arthur Williams, who had years of experience in a book bindery and who was taking over much of the routine of my job. I told Alfred that I had time for some other work, that if I was to stay with him I did not want to be confined to production. His answer was to fire Williams and give me a green assistant from the bookkeeping department. That was the handwriting on the wall.

Early in 1925 I announced that I was leaving. I offered to tell Alfred why and he said he would ask me sometime, but he never did. I had only the slightest contact with him for forty-five or fifty years, but after his second marriage to a woman everyone loved and who brought out Alfred's humanity, we finally became friends. Time had changed us both, of course. I found in him traits that were no doubt suppressed when he was young. His politics were more liberal than I expected and support of the national parks had become one of his great enthusiasms. I very much regretted our years of estrangement. On September 20, 1980, we had a modest celebration on the sixtieth anniversary of the day I began work in his office.

The years I spent at Knopf's were a splendid substitute for a foregone college education. Added to what I learned from my work was the opportunity to know and observe dozens of writers, to be exposed to their ideas, to examine their places in the world.

My personal dealings with most of those writers was chiefly as the slave of their publisher. I worked with them on proofs, and, when they were interested, discussed the design of their books. I felt that I was part of the 1920s literary ferment, and New York was the center of it. New writers and critics were coming forward, and new small publishing houses were making them known. A decade later the Great Depression was to cool much of this excitement, but I was there during the height of it.

The only Knopf author who really became a friend was Henry Mencken. Our office was his New York base, both as correspondent for the *Baltimore Sun* papers and later as editor of the *American Mercury*, which Knopf published. In 1924 he covered the famous six-week, 103-ballot Democratic convention, a stalemate between Al Smith, Irish-Catholic candidate of the antiprohibition people, and the antiliquor, anti-Catholic backers of William McAdoo, who was Woodrow Wilson's son-in-law. This was a story made to order for Mencken, and he brought splendid firsthand reports back to the office. He called McAdoo's supporters people from the Bible Belt and swore that they believed the Pope had a bomb under each of their seats at the convention. He encouraged me to crash the show, to see the spectacle of hundreds of sweating delegates suffering on the below-ground floor of the old Madison Square Garden while urban and rural politicians fought for the soul of their party.

Mencken was a stimulating friend for a young man, and I was lucky to know him. We corresponded for years, exchanging choice bits of what he called Americana, examples of the foolishness or vulgarity of some of our contemporaries as expressed in pseudo-patriotic songs, fatuous speeches, and corny advertising. One of his observations which I like to remember is this: "An idealist is one who, on noticing that a rose smells better than a cabbage, concludes that it will also make better soup."

My last encounter with him turned out to be embarrassing. One of my jobs after Knopf's was reviewing extraliterary publications for the *Bookman*, an old magazine which had recently been bought by a dilettante named Seward Collins. Collins asked to meet Mencken, and I arranged it. Soon after that the *Bookman* ran a long series of essays by Collins defending a group of once-influential Princeton humanists and attacking Mencken and other critics who did not share Collins's reactionary social enthusiasms. I don't suppose this bothered Mencken at all, but I felt I had somehow betrayed him.

I knew Mencken when he was at his best, and his later political opinions troubled me, especially his hatred of Franklin Roosevelt and all he stood for. Mencken had allowed his early contempt for small-town illiteracy and bigotry to develop into an elitism scornful of programs to improve the public welfare. These programs also tried to raise the level of American education, which he himself had always lamented, but consistency was never one of his virtues.

In his diaries, published long after his death, critics found evidence of anti-Semitism. I never saw any of this when I knew him. Above conventional politeness, he was not one to be squeamish about commenting on Jews he knew. He had strong reactions to them, as to everyone else. His long friendships with many Jews and his well-known contempt for bigots lead me to believe that the charge of anti-Semitism only arose when many of his favorite targets had disappeared and it had become fashionable in some circles to sneer at him.

The first year I worked at Knopf's I lived with my family in Hartsdale. My mother felt less isolated there than in Flushing, but there was one cruel disappointment. They wanted to join the Sunningdale Country Club, to which most of their friends belonged. Some time in the past my father had somehow made an enemy of an influential member of that club, a man whose truculence matched his own, and Father's application was blackballed. This may seem a trivial thing, but in their circles the country club was the social center, and the rejection was traumatic.

When I resumed living with them, I found that relations with my father were as stormy as ever. Small disagreements became big emotional arguments. One recurrent fight was over catching the morning train to the city. I was supposed to drive to the station with him, and he was in a fury every time I was not ready to leave exactly when he was. Dissension about the use of the family automobile was another source of strife, but most of the quarrels were even more petty, and I cannot now remember how they started. I was out of school and holding down a job, and I resented his efforts to treat me like a child. My mother was under constant pressure to keep the peace, but she could not win. If the kitchen was out of his favorite A1 Steak Sauce, it became a major offense against him.

After a year, the end of their third in Hartsdale, my parents managed to afford to move back to our old Manhattan house on West 77th Street. They wanted to end the commuting struggle, and they wanted my sister, Marian, then approaching sixteen, to circulate among the children of their city friends. This was late in 1921. I lived with them there for about five years. Toward the end of 1925 I left Knopf's and started work as a free-lance designer. Although I was getting a good start, I considered a full-time job with Horace Liveright, a brilliant erratic publisher reputed to conduct a racy salon in the apartment above his offices. I also had serious talks with Longmans Green, of London, about taking charge of production in their New York office.

These prospects made me realize that if I took another full-time job I would again be tied down. I wanted to see a little of the world, so I took a few hundred dollars I had inherited and sailed off to see some of Europe. As I hoped, the trip was a tremendous educational experience. I decided that traveling alone was the best way to cover the most places in the shortest time. I had friends on shipboard and I joined others now and then, but I was free to set my own schedule.

It was a typical young man's grand tour of museums, churches, cafés, and streets—everything I could see in cities from Venice and Budapest in the south and east to Berlin, Amsterdam, and London in the north and west, with Paris in between. I found I had retained a fluent command of German from my governess days (with a twelve-year-old's vocabulary) and a serviceable amount of French from school, which made traveling easier. Besides all these cultural and sentimental experiences, I found time to pursue a beautiful, passionate, and resolutely virginal young American woman called Timmie Babcock who was traveling with one of my old Scarsdale friends.

I visited my grandfather's birthplace in tiny Ludwigslust and saw the family name over their store. My great uncle, in his eighties, had resumed practicing law after the war and was supporting the family there. Germany had just gone through a catastrophic currency inflation, and I made a small collection of worthless million-mark bank notes and ceramic coins. One of my female cousins had

On board ship, 1926

just gone to China from Ludwigslust. China had escaped the war, and opportunities for young women seemed better there. I also visited a relative whom I had known well as a music teacher in New York; she had returned to Europe to marry another cousin in Hamburg. They were the only relatives I knew personally who later disappeared in the Holocaust.

Besides what I brought home in my head, I acquired a few small pictures and artifacts which I kept for the rest of my life. Home from my trip, I lived with my family for another six months. Then my father's health broke down, he gave up his business, and the family moved to a small apartment. By that time I could afford a place of my own. I found a fifth-floor walk-up apartment on 51st Street west of Fifth Avenue, near the theaters and other attractions of the city.

I was finally really independent, and it was a relief to leave the endless battles with my father. I knew my mother was relieved, too, even though she was losing the comfort she got from the presence of her favorite child. Where she for years had to cope with my father's aggressive behavior, she now had to deal with his poor health and the loss of his business.

Leaving my family home virtually ended my connections with the people I had grown up with and with whom I no longer shared goals and tastes and life-styles. I was making a niche for myself in the publishing industry, and my new living arrangements were a significant token of my new life.

4 🍎 Free-Lance Designer

What impelled me at the age of twenty-two to try to make a living as a free-lance book production man and designer when the custom in the industry was to have that work done in-house?

By the time I left my job as production manager for Knopf in the fall of 1925, I had acquired substantial skills but did not know what I wanted to do with them. At Knopf I witnessed the eternal conflict between art and profits and was not at all sure that I wanted to stay there. As it turned out, my five-year stint with Knopf was my first and last full-time job.

Before I left Knopf I was asked to help with the production of the first six books of a new firm named the Viking Press, started by George Oppenheimer and Harold Guinzburg. George was a former Knopf employee, a frivolous and pretentious fellow whom I detested for his constant boasts about his place in what he called "Jewish Society." Harold supplied the capital and business sense for the enterprise, as well as a more serious interest in literature. George soon flew off to Hollywood, where he was more at home. Benjamin Huebsch, a talented but struggling small publisher, joined Harold and brought with him a valuable string of authors and also someone experienced in production.

Making those books for Viking gave me the idea that I might be able to make a living as a free lance, available to help new publishers with the production of their books. There were several of these new houses, usually started by an editor and a salesperson, who could not afford to hire an experienced production person. This turned out to be a good notion, and I got work from several of these firms, Random House, Simon and Schuster, and some others. I visited most of the publishing offices in New York, elegant with a bowler hat and walking stick—an affectation not as outrageous then as it would be today.

Designing the book is part of the production process of course, and as my confidence grew I began to call myself a book designer. I was the first person to work as a free-lance designer for trade book and educational book publishers. It was a good time to get started. Some of the new houses were interested in using good design to mark the quality of their publications and to attract authors. My former boss, Alfred Knopf, was making his competitors think more about the appearance of their books.

What do book designers really do? Many people have asked me that question. I usually answer that they do for a book what an architect does for a house. Their job is to devise a physical object that will convey the author's mood and ideas to the reader, just as architects try to suit the personalities, habits, customs, and practical needs of their clients within the limitations of the site, building codes, and budget.

Book designers select the type and paper; plan the page, the margins, and arrangement of any illustrations; and design the title page, chapter heads, and other typographic elements. They choose the size and shape of the book—what is called the format—and the binding materials. They design the binding and frequently the paper jacket. And they have a budget to meet.

The first and most important decision the typographer makes is the choice of types for a piece of printing. There are hundreds of typefaces, and the typographer must be acquainted with most of them. Many of their differences are minute and subtle, but to the designer who knows them they speak eloquently and can embody the ideas and moods of authors.

Even a limited treatise on type design can be as long as this book; I can only try to emphasize here how much the effect of a piece of printing depends on the sensitive choice of type. This

THE EMBRYOLOGICAL TREATISES
of
HIERONYMUS FABRICIUS
Of Aquapendente

The Formation of the Egg and of the Chick
(De Formatione Ovi et Pulli)

The Formed Fetus   italics
(De Formato Foetu)

A Facsimile Edition
With an Introduction, a Translation,
and a Commentary
BY
HOWARD B. ADELMANN
Professor of Histology and Embriology
Cornell University

Ithaca, New York
CORNELL UNIVERSITY PRESS
1 9 4 2

The Embryological Treatises of
HIERONYMUS FABRICIUS
of Aquapendente

THE FORMATION OF THE EGG AND OF
THE CHICK   [*De Formatione Ovi et Pulli*]

THE FORMED FETUS   [*De Formato Foetu*]

A FACSIMILE EDITION, WITH AN INTRODUCTION, A TRANSLATION,
AND A COMMENTARY BY HOWARD B. ADELMANN
PROFESSOR OF HISTOLOGY AND EMBRYOLOGY, CORNELL UNIVERSITY

Ithaca, New York : Cornell University Press : 1942

Although the foregoing description applies to all animals, it happens, however, that these vessels vary in position in different species. Indeed, in the human fetus the umbilical vessels ** are scattered and disseminated through the fetal side of a large, cake-like fleshy mass. When they leave this and proceed toward the fetus, they become very long, unbranched, intertwined, venous and arterial trunks.†† In the dog and cat the same vessels likewise extend and branch throughout a fleshy substance resembling a girdle; ‡‡ and when they leave it, short trunks result which proceed toward the fetus. But in cattle §§ and sheep ¶¶ the umbilical vessels branch and extend not only throughout the fleshy substance, but especially outside of it, for only the ends of the vessels and the smallest fibers are received by the fleshy substance. But, in whatever way these vessels are distributed, they are always, nevertheless, connected with and supported by one membrane called the chorion (as I shall relate in the proper place), to which they adhere. I may add that the fetuses of the ox and sheep * especially have the umbilical vessels scattered throughout this membrane.

But since I have mentioned the fleshy substance, let us now discuss it.

Margin:
** Figs. 6,B; 9,C; 10,A; 16,D,E.
[4]
†† Figs. 9,C; 10,A; 11,B.
‡‡ Figs. 53,C; 56,C.
§§ Fig. 42,D.
¶¶ Figs. 28,B; 29,B; 31,B.
* Fig. 28,C; 29,C.

The umbilical vessels of the dog and cat.

How the umbilical vessels of the ox and sheep are distributed.

CHAPTER III.   The Fleshy Substance

IN THE FIRST PLACE, on the internal surface of the uterus of almost all viviparous animals, there may be seen a certain fleshy substance¹ which is applied to, or spread and poured over the ends of the vessels which extend to the uterus. In almost all animals it is uniform in color, softness, openness or looseness of texture, and thickness, but it differs considerably in size, position, shape, and in the number of its parts, and is by no means to be reckoned among the investments of the fetus.

This is that flesh which Galen² speaks of as "glandular fleshes fused with the vessels of the uterus,"³ and in the first book of his *De semine,* chapter 7,⁴ he refers to it as "fleshes which are observed to be deposited around the orifices of the vessels in some animals." In book XV of his *De usu partium,* chapter 4,⁴ he says that in all animals which are given to jumping, like deer and goats, extensions of the umbilical vessels are connected to the uterus not only by thin membranes⁵ but also by viscous flesh resembling a sort of fat.

Margin: *What Galen's "glandular flesh fused with the uterus" is.*

---

[1]   THE FORMATION OF THE EGG
AND OF THE CHICK BY HIERONYMUS

FABRICIUS OF AQUAPENDENTE, *Anatomist of Padua*

PART I.   THE FORMATION OF THE EGGS
OF BIRDS

CHAPTER I.   Description of the Uteri of the Bird

MY discussion of the formation of the fetus follows immediately upon my treatment of the semen, since the semen is produced for the very reason that the fetus may be formed from it. ||Now the fetuses of animals arise, some from eggs,

Margin: *The fetus may be formed in*

---

[1]   THE FORMED FETUS BY HIERONYMUS

FABRICIUS OF AQUAPENDENTE, *Anatomist of Padua*

PART I.   THE DISSECTION OR DESCRIPTION
OF THE PARTS OF THE FETUS

CHAPTER I.

I HAVE FOUND it convenient to divide my discussion of generation into three parts. The first deals with the generation and instruments of the semen; the second considers the nature and faculties of the semen after it has been produced, that is to say, the generation and forma-

Margin: *The author divides his treatise on generation into three parts.*

Pages from Fabricius's Embryological Treatises demonstrating how a typographer works: typed copy for the title page, finished title page, part titles, chapter openings, and a typical text page

type, furthermore, must be suitable for printing on the paper to be used. Ink and paper can modify type; it is the letter as printed which the reader sees.

To take a number of words and arrange them in a pattern which is both beautiful and makes clear the meaning and relative value of each word can be one of the most satisfying of all creative acts. Every layout cannot be a work of art, but it can show taste and order. All copy does not offer equal opportunities for interesting layouts; usually the more words the more opportunity. A title page that includes only a short title and the author's and publisher's names is more difficult to make interesting, perhaps, than one with a long title, a subtitle, and editors' names. This also applies to the design of the chapter titles and other elements.

Printing design has gone through many mutations since the invention of movable types in the fifteenth century. Movable types are single letters, usually metal, which are assembled (the word is "composed") to make words and pages and then can be recomposed and used again. Printed books were first intended to look like handwritten ones, but soon new type designs and new printing presses produced new styles. In what we call modern (post-Renaissance) times, printing design has quickly followed styles in architecture, clothing, vehicles, and new ideas in painting, philosophy, and history. When I first began to think about design in the twenties, most current books still reflected the nineteenth-century fascination with new machinery. Typefaces were mechanical and ungraceful, ornamentation was disdained. There were signs of change, however.

In 1890, near the end of his life, the English poet and artist William Morris founded the Kelmscott Press. His lifelong crusade for a socialist society was rooted in the belief that a revival of craftsmanship would be the salvation of the British worker, and the press was the last of his many handicraft ventures. He found that his high standards for materials and construction produced books that only the rich could buy, a conflict with his socialist ideals he could not resolve.

His emphasis on craftsmanship stimulated a revival of good printing, but his taste for Gothic types and elaborate decoration had only a limited influence on the style of current books. Younger designers were soon turning away from the extravagance of Morris's style, and he himself said before he died, "I have spent a vast

STEEL PLATES

AND THEIR FABRICATION

A REFERENCE BOOK ON PLATES AND

PLATE PRODUCTS FOR ENGINEERS,

DRAFTSMEN, AND FABRICATORS

Lukens Steel Company AND SUBSIDIARIES

BY-PRODUCTS STEEL CORPORATION · LUKENWELD, INC.

323 LUKENS BUILDING, COATESVILLE, PENNSYLVANIA

CABLE ADDRESS: LUKENS

Type and austere layout to suggest products of the steel mill amount of time designing furniture and wall-papers, carpets and curtains, but after all I am inclined to think that sort of thing is mostly rubbish, and would prefer to live with the plainest white-washed walls and wooden chairs and tables."

The movement to improve typography and book decoration in the twentieth century developed first in the limited or special edition, then in esoteric nonfiction, then in novels and textbooks, and finally in the paperback. This progression, in inverse ratio to the social value of the books treated, followed the cultural trickle-down which we have also seen in architecture and the other arts. It was a familiar paradox of our democratic society, and if Morris had lived to see it, he would not have been at all surprised.

After World War I the defeated and impoverished Germans, reaching for Western business, moved away from their traditional

illt fein und ihre Bereitwilligfeit dafür auch

black letter and began to employ the Latin-style alphabet used by the rest of the Western world in trade and in literature. A brilliant group of artists at the Bauhaus in Dessau, Germany, were working to integrate design in architecture, furniture, printing, manufactures, and apparatus of all kinds in what was called the International Style. Leaders in type design and typography, they produced many new typefaces consistent with their theories. Sold abroad, these types stimulated innovation first in advertising design and then in books. During World War II many Bauhaus people came to America and added to the impact of their ideas by their work here.

The Nazis looked on modern ideas in art as dangerous, a threat to their political agenda. The use of the Latin letter was outlawed, first in army publications, then in all printing, and a return to the "truly German" black letter was decreed. Happily, this era of political art ended with the rest of Nazi *kultur*, and the enormous influence of Bauhaus ideas was not lost.

It was inevitable that I should welcome modern concepts in design. I had always thought of myself as a construction person. As an amateur carpenter I had looked for ways to shortcut conventional trade practices and simplify structure. The ideas of the Bauhaus in Germany, relating design in every field to an emphasis on structure in architecture, had a powerful influence on me. It seemed obvious that logic, not custom, should determine the placement of elements in any design.

I remember with pleasure an encounter with a country-club-type publisher-client. He looked at my layout for a title page and said, "You know, Bob, I have never liked those asymmetrical layouts." I asked him whether the front door of his house was in the center, and I never had any trouble with him after that.

In 1940 I said in a speech: "Almost any piece of design, if honestly conceived and competently executed, will reflect the social outlook of the designer. Whether house or bridge, sculpture or mural, vehicle or textile, cutlery or printing, his work will in some measure suggest the sort of world he wants to see around him. Today humanity wants order—order in its economy and order in its government, order in its cities and order in its homes. A taste for frills and gingerbread, a yearning for period styles, is all too often the mark of the escapist and reactionary. The designer's first job today is to help bring order and repose into our troubled world. Let him keep his eye on this ball, and the customers will respond with the proper aesthetic reactions."

That statement defines what I was trying to do fifty years ago and what I have tried to do ever since: to shape for myself, as far as I could, in design, in social relations, in government, in land-use, the sort of world I want to live in. My words may seem dated now as postmodernism brings back period styles, but the argument is being heard again. I have always been contemptuous of the familiar statement that "there is no accounting for taste." It seems obvious that one's preferences are clearly the result of temperament, experience, perception, knowledge, and social ideas. To be unable or unwilling to see this seems to me to be obtuse and insensitive.

The 1930s saw a sham battle between the so-called traditional and the so-called modern. New conceptions menaced the comfortable eclecticism of many designers, the escapism of book collectors, the inertia of the monopoly American Typefounders Co., and the belated investment of typesetting machine makers in revivals of seventeenth- and eighteenth-century faces. By the start of World War II the sham battle was over, and I am happy to boast that I had a part in ending it. The acceptance of modernism did not of

CONNECTICUT

CLOCKMAKERS

OF THE

EIGHTEENTH CENTURY

PENROSE R. HOOPES

HARTFORD, CONN.: EDWIN VALENTINE MITCHELL

NEW YORK: DODD, MEAD & COMPANY

1930

Typography suggesting the engraving on clock faces

course mean that everyone who embraced it really understood its basic ideas. In 1951 an exhibition sponsored by the Institute of Graphic Arts' Book Clinic impelled me to circulate an open letter which I quote at length because it illustrates this confusion.

"I have just been to see the Trade Book Clinic's interesting five-man show called Books For Our Time. This exhibition is described as 'a permanent and enlightening record of an important phase in the development—the physical evolution—of the book . . . [demonstrating] that we now have a new set of standards, as valid for our time as the early printer's were for his.'

"The exhibition committee was Marshall Lee, chairman, Merle Armitage, John Begg, S. A. Jacobs, and Ernst Reichl. The show contains no text or technical books or children's books. There are 14 European and 138 American books, issued since 1900. In the published catalog, Mr. Lee explains '. . . the committee feels that this number is in fair proportion to Europe's part in the modern movement.'

"How many of you saw the exhibition? What did you think of it? Are any of you shocked by the impropriety of five designers selecting 84 of their own books, 36 of them published since 1948, for a half-century exhibition which includes but 138 American titles? Are you alarmed because the organizer of this petty scandal is now Chairman of the Clinic? Are you embarrassed because a president of the Institute is one of the five artists involved?

"Well, what do you expect? For twenty-five years typographers have been trying to free book design from the sterile period-printing of the little private press and the big limited edition, have been trying to develop a style based on twentieth-century ideas and methods. For twenty-five years the Institute has carefully ignored this work, has accepted no responsibility for leadership in this effort to move forward, has furnished no criticism, has established no standards except those implied by the selections and rejections in the catch-as-catch-can Fifty Books competitions. . . .

"Five designers, assisted by no independent student or critic, assembled the show. Mr. Lee explains: 'Rather than this being a case of the committee's selecting its own books, it was that the designers of the most contemporary books had been selected to be on the committee. . . .'

"What then is lacking in the exhibition? Objectivity, of course—and therefore also completeness, variety, balance—and therefore authority. Because the five designers are all fascinated by the typographic stunt, we have a show consisting mostly of stunts: a complete catalog of the standard stunts which have become the type flowers of 1950, and a large group of individual stunts which by themselves, frankly labeled, would make a pleasant show.

"The printed remarks of the committee members pay lip service to the principles of modern design: order, directness, simplicity; respect for form of letter and function of page; avoidance of useless ornamentation. Their selections suggest, however, that these principles really do not appeal very much to these men. Apparently they agree largely with Mr. Lee, who writes: 'It is not enough for the designer to be "unobtrusive." In dealing with a literature aiming at the subconscious almost more than at the conscious mind, the mechanical neutrality of the printer's craft is a positive detriment. The book designer must now participate actively in the author's attempt. . . .'

"This highly subjective approach, however, is only one way to go about designing a book. Some of the 38 other designers represented by 68 books in this show, and some of the many others not represented at all, are more willing to accept the traditional discipline of the printer's craft, and find it no handicap to developing new forms.

"Has the Institute muffed the ball? Are you Directors satisfied that our first 'modern' show should be advertised as definitive and should turn out to be so limited? The question is not whether the exhibition committee is made up of adventurers or of missionaries, or even whether their exhibition will advance at all the development of a twentieth-century style. The question is whether the Institute is satisfied with its own contribution; whether this will be our last, as it is our first, effort to stimulate the contemporary designer, or whether we will finally act with authority to discharge our responsibilities to our own time."

I received thirty or forty replies to my open letter, some from people working in fields quite remote from book design. None of them disagreed with my contentions; even the five men responsible for the exhibition seemed chastened by the criticism voiced in several public meetings called to discuss my letter. Ripples from the stone I had dropped into the pool of Institute complacency continued to spread.

I was always chiefly interested in the mass-produced book manufactured in unlimited editions in large printing houses and binderies. In about thirty years of working for all kinds of publishers, most of my books were made in these large plants. I found that some of them could hold their own in competitive exhibitions beside the output of smaller shops with reputations for quality work.

For some years I was the only free-lance person offering publishers both design and production services, meeting the needs of new publishers such as Viking, Simon and Schuster, and Random House. Sooner than I expected, I also began to get commissions from older and larger firms who had well-staffed production departments but wanted some change in the appearance of their books.

Working for many publishers, I had a chance to design a great variety of books. At one end of the price scale was Modern Age Books, established by Richard Storrs Childs in 1937 to publish low-priced paperbacks. Their list was excellent but their business skills limited, and they did not survive. Pocket Books, started later and built on the experience and mistakes of Modern Age, is often given credit for being the first paperback publishing house in America, but that is not the true story.

I must confess that some of the first books I made in the twenties were not always faithful to my own principles of functional design. I was guilty of indulging the taste of some of my clients for elaborate decoration, especially in the Vinal books and in certain of the profitable limited editions. I owned some type and an assortment of type ornament, which consists of small decorative elements frequently based on flowers or foliage that can be composed like type as part of a design. I used it on some title pages and bindings which I set by hand in my studio. Times were prosperous, and there was a growing market for elegant, frequently limited, editions. Random House, one of my early clients, was a leader in importing such books and later in producing them in America. Their success led others into this field, and these books became big business in the thirties. Typical of the innocent customers for such cultural chic was a newly prosperous press-agent acquaintance of mine who said, "If you see any limited editions I should have, buy them for me."

A successful exploiter of these customers was George Macy, proprietor of the Limited Editions Club. His taste exactly reflected that of my press-agent friend. He combined the work of well-known writers, illustrators, and designers without much concern for the appropriateness of the match; the names were what sold the books. I designed for him an edition of O. Henry's *The Voice of the City* with full-color illustrations by the German expressionist George Grosz. It was printed by offset lithography in the

ALMANAC
for New Yorkers
1938

ACCOMMODATED TO THE FIVE BOROUGHS
BUT MAY WITHOUT SENSIBLE ERROR
SERVE FOR THE ENTIRE METROPOLITAN DIS-
TRICT AND EVEN MORE DISTANT POINTS

Compiled by the Workers of the Federal Writers'
Project of the Works Progress Administration
in the City of New York

WITH ILLUSTRATIONS BY THE WPA FEDERAL ART PROJECT
IN THE CITY OF NEW YORK

SPONSORED BY THE GUILDS' COMMITTEE FOR
FEDERAL WRITERS' PUBLICATIONS, INC.

MODERN AGE BOOKS INC., NEW YORK

A very early paperback

shop of my Danish inventor friend Hugo Knudsen. It was a tech-
nically successful piece of book artisanship, but the illustrations
were quite unsuited to O. Henry's stories. Fortunately, this did not
trouble Grosz.

Another of my early clients, Covici-Friede, catered to this trade
with naive erotic works by obscure European writers. I must say
that I enjoyed devising fancy typography and decoration to fit the

December

Shares with nine other months the distinction of getting more wind from the Northwest than from any other direction. That's enough of a distinction for a month that has Christmas.

4 SUNDAY. *Point to Remember: A single Health Department clinic alone issues working certificates to about 12,000 New York child-workers every year* * * * This day in 1914 Henry Ford's Peace Ship *Oscar II* sailed from New York for Europe.

5 MONDAY. *The First District Dental Society is very likely to be meeting this week* * * * What is supposed to have been the first velocipede riding school in the land was opened this day in 1868 at 932 Broadway * * * Three men organized the American League for Physical Culture, the first nudist group, this day in 1929.

6 TUESDAY. *Finnish Independence Day* * * * Probably the first American "Merchants of Death" were three respectable New Netherland business men who were caught selling firearms to the Indians in the winter of 1647–1648. Against his better judgment, Stuyvesant did not execute them, but confiscated all their property instead.

7 WEDNESDAY. *Delaware Day* * * * This day in 1917 the United States declared war on Austria-Hungary.

People rarely contract chills
Who spend their time in bars and grills.
T. S.

98

rococo style of these authors. This firm also published more serious books. Pascal (Pat) Covici, the editor with whom I worked, was a friend of John Steinbeck and published several of his early unprofitable novels, which I designed. After Covici-Friede was no more, Pat joined the Viking Press, and Steinbeck's *The Grapes of Wrath* became a sensational success, but Viking was not then one of my clients.

THE POEMS OF
CATULLUS

TRANSLATED BY HORACE GREGORY

WITH DRAWINGS BY ZHENYA GAY

COVICI·FRIEDE, INC., PUBLISHERS

NEW YORK, MCMXXXI

Type and layout to suit the illustration

Type ornament, set by myself, and design suggesting the sentimental nature of the poems

A unique client for whom I made many books was Harold Vinal, a poet-publisher made immortal in E. E. Cummings's poem "Beauty Hurts Harold Vinal." He was what is called a vanity publisher, issuing books for which the authors paid the costs of production and promotion. He was a handsome, effeminate man, with

THE TWO SPIES

NATHAN HALE *and*
ROBERT TOWNSEND

BY MORTON PENNYPACKER

BOSTON AND NEW YORK
HOUGHTON MIFFLIN COMPANY
The Riverside Press Cambridge
1930

Typography suggesting well-printed eighteenth-century books

THE TWO SPIES

NATHAN HALE

LATE IN the evening of September 22, 1776, Captain John Montressor, of the British Engineers, who was serving as aide-de-camp to Lord Howe, appeared under flag of truce at the American outposts on Harlem Plains, New York. He bore a letter to General Washington respecting the exchange of prisoners. General Putnam, Captain Alexander Hamilton, and Captain William Hull were among those who met him. To them Montressor verbally gave the information that an American officer, one Captain Hale, had been executed that morning as a spy. It was startling news, and to Hull it came like a shock, for Nathan Hale had been his chum at college* and confided to him details of the dangerous mission he had undertaken. A week later, the sad news reached the home of Hale, and one of his brothers, Enoch, started for the en-

* In the class of 1773 at Yale College among others were Nathan Hale and his brother Enoch, Benjamin Tallmadge, and William Townsend. William Hull was in the class of 1772.

a charming voice and manner but humorous and unpretentious. The women at the Poetry Society loved to hear him read verse, and that brought him many manuscripts. He exploited the style of his books, and I enjoyed designing them in spite of the often banal content. Harold's parents came from Vinalhaven, Maine. I learned that they had not spoken to each other for twenty years, except in public. After a few years and dozens of books published, Harold eloped with the son of one of his favorite authors, the business folded, and I lost a good account.

Most of my other clients were personally less fascinating than Vinal but more serious about literature. I designed books for Houghton Mifflin, in Boston, for some years, but Mr. Houghton did not like to acknowledge that they might need outside help, so I was never introduced to him. Edwin Valentine Mitchell, a bookseller and occasional publisher in Hartford, was one of my favorite patrons. Each of his books was unique, offering me a special challenge, and he and his associates were delightful people to work with.

One of Mitchell's books was *Noravind*, an account of a trip along the edge of the Norwegian ice in a sealing ship, written by Dudley Vaill Talcott, owner of the ship. Dudley's relatives were business leaders and diplomats; he was the family eccentric, a sculptor and an adventurer, married to the beautiful daughter of the sealing ship's captain. I visited them at his mother's house in Hartford. Mrs. Talcott was a sophisticated and cultivated old woman who kept a cow in her large city backyard as her family, the Hookers, had done since the founding of the city in the early seventeenth century. Dudley was a friend for forty years.

A client of mine for ten years was the leading American publisher of Marxist books, International Publishers, directed by an erudite Russian named Alexander Trachtenberg. It continued to issue books through the worst of the anti-Soviet hysteria of the McCarthy period and is still in business.

Among other clients were G.P. Putnam's Sons and their affiliates Coward-McCann and John Day, and the Macauley Company, for whom I designed a landmark series of annuals on general culture called *The American Caravan*. Another was Warder Norton's small company on which he left the mark of his strong personal tastes and high standards and which later became, under Donald Lamm, large, independent, and employee-owned.

THE ART OF
JAPANESE
GARDENS

by Loraine E. Kuck

THE JOHN DAY COMPANY, NEW YORK

Type and layout to suit the illustration

I also produced books for a number of university presses, including Columbia, Harvard, Cornell, Syracuse, and Louisiana State. These were usually serious works of scholarship, interesting to work on and often requiring innovative typographic treatment. They also had more generous production budgets, enabling me to use better paper and binding materials.

I frequently received commissions from outside the printing and publishing industry from museums, government agencies, and trade associations. A steel mill commissioned a technical manual, and I once designed a whiskey label for a distiller. I was occasionally asked to produce a privately printed book; this I did under the name of the Beekman Hill Press, an imprint I invented.

Several printers hired me to design books for their customers. Chief among these was the J. J. Little and Ives Co. in New York. This was a big printing house and book bindery built up in the 1880s by Joseph J. Little, a major figure in city education circles and in public affairs. His son Arthur, who headed the business when I worked there, was a different sort, seriously devoted to social climbing. Once he had me design a book about a cruise the Littles took on Hamilton Twombly's yacht. Written by Mrs. T's social secretary, it described high life at sea and was presented to their hosts as a token of the Littles' gratitude. Because Arthur Little had been a lieutenant colonel in World War I, he made an attempt to duplicate Teddy Roosevelt's political rise from the army to the White House. He set up a campaign office at the printing plant, with an old-pro political manager whose cynical talk I relished. They inflated an expensive trial balloon which disappeared into the ether at the 1936 Republican convention.

Unfortunately for my personal relations with the colonel, my grandmother Josephy recalled that as a young bachelor my grandfather had been a boarder in the home of the J. J. Littles. When the colonel learned that I knew that his own parents had not been above keeping a boarder and that my Jewish grandparents had been entertained by them later, he never forgave me.

Little and Ives was a good shop; J. J. Little's standards survived his son's follies, and I was able to produce excellent books there. Some of these were published by my own clients, others were jobs sold by Little's salespeople with a stipulation that I would be designing them. One advantage for me in working there was in being able to go into the plant and discuss the typesetting and presswork directly with the employees. I urged the management to display the finished books where the people who made them could see what they had accomplished, but the executives could not see any reason for doing that.

It was good to find so many publishers who could and would use my services. Many were small houses whose staffs lacked the skills I could provide. They gave me an opportunity to work on many different kinds of books. What I wanted, in addition, was to design books for older, larger firms who could produce books efficiently but would want to buy my taste and ideas. My first opening of that kind came during my second year as a free lance.

5 🍎 *Harcourt to Stieglitz*

In 1926 I went to see Donald Brace, whom I had met one evening at Alfred Knopf's house in Purchase, New York. He asked me to design an edition of Giovanni Papini's *Life of Christ*. Harcourt, Brace and Company had sold twenty-seven printings in four years and wanted a new, more elegant edition. After I completed that project, Brace asked me whether I would like to design all their trade books. I suggested a monthly fee; he called it too low, and I gave in gracefully. My work for Harcourt, Brace lasted for over twenty-five years and was the most satisfying of all my experiences with publishers.

Harcourt, Brace was not an old company. Founded in 1919, it had grown rapidly and in a few years had established a position comparable to nineteenth-century pillars of the industry. Having it as a client gave me a solid base for my new career and confidence to promote my ideas about printing practice and design.

Brace was a quiet, old-school gentleman with impeccable taste who cared as much about literature as he did about money. Alfred Harcourt was a more flamboyant personality, skilled in attracting writers. He was less reserved than Brace in dealing with employees, was a notorious pincher of unwary secretaries, and was also guardedly anti-Semitic. He was clearly unwilling to employ Jews, but he flattered me (and also his own pretense at liberalism) by telling me he did not know I was Jewish. He was quite willing, however, to profit from the work of many successful Jewish writers such as Louis Untermeyer and Lewis Mumford.

Luckily, I actually had little contact with Harcourt because production was one of Brace's responsibilities. He maintained a relaxed atmosphere in which I was able to do a great deal of my best work. This was made easier by Howard Clark, the production manager, through whom my layouts and specifications were transformed into books. Clark had none of the fear, which I sometimes encountered elsewhere, that my being engaged as designer was a reflection on his own capacities.

Harcourt, Brace was a training ground for several young editors who later were important figures in publishing. I especially enjoyed my association with Chester Kerr, who became director of the Yale University Press, and Robert Giroux, who as I write is still an active partner in Farrar Straus and Giroux, one of the last large, really independent publishers.

I spent many days in the Harcourt, Brace office. This gave me time to discuss with authors details about design. My job was to make the physical form of their books reflect what they were thinking and saying. When they had good visual sense they would give me valuable comments and useful ideas—some, however, had little interest in graphic expression. In the case of William Saroyan, his only concern was to urge me to use larger type for his name on the title page of one of his novels.

At the end of my years with Harcourt, Brace I designed many textbooks. I was encouraged to make high school books into better teaching tools that were also more attractive to students. One editor I worked with was William Jovanovich. Bill's father was a Yugoslav coal miner in Indiana, and when I knew him he still retained a lot of his father's radical ideas. He was imaginative and energetic. After both Harcourt and Brace had died, two pedestrian textbook managers had terms as president of the company, and then Bill succeeded them. Many years later he was the head of Harcourt Brace Jovanovich, which for a time owned amusement parks, insurance companies, and other hardly literary properties.

Working on textbooks, I got an enlightening view of how publishers catered to the most benighted political ideas of school-

An effort to suggest the intimacy of this book

book buyers. Even Harcourt, Brace, which published the works of many liberal authors, was not above shaping the texts of secondary schoolbooks to conform to the ideologies of school authorities in Texas.

Editors were expected to go along quietly. I designed an updated edition of a very profitable Harcourt, Brace high school his-

FOOD
AND DRINK

BY LOUIS UNTERMEYER

WITH DRAWINGS BY GEORGE PLANK

HARCOURT, BRACE AND COMPANY

NEW YORK

Type and layout to suit the illustration

tory, *The Rise of American Democracy*. The editor was James M. Reid, with whom I worked on many textbooks and thought of as a friend. He was a self-proclaimed liberal with a photo of civil rights leader Roger Baldwin on his desk, but he did not allow his liberal attitudes to affect the books he edited. *The Rise of American*

Democracy, for example, showed a limited concern for real democracy. It managed to avoid even mentioning fascism, the most anti-democratic movement seen in the twentieth century. In the few paragraphs it devoted to the labor movement, it failed to mention that the rise of industrial unionism was a milestone in the rise of American democracy.

In spite of occasional disputes about the content of books, which was not really supposed to be my concern at all, I enjoyed producing educational books. I found their frequently complicated structure challenging, compared to the simpler requirements of most trade book manuscripts.

Some textbooks did present an irksome problem. It was the custom for publishers of successful high school books to issue new editions every few years. These were intended to look quite different from previous editions and sometimes borrowed a few design ideas from competing publications. I was not very good at that kind of sleight of hand. Once I had used my skills and imagination to solve a design problem in the best way I could, I found it very difficult to solve it again in another way just in order to produce something different. It was not a matter of artistic integrity or any such elevated concern, it was simply that having once done my best, the second effort could only be second best. I would have to resort to a variety of typographic tricks, and the original challenge would be gone.

One of my most successful Harcourt, Brace books was Carl Sandburg's *Steichen the Photographer*. Sandburg, a poet and biographer with an international reputation, was frequently at the Harcourt, Brace office. He was the brother-in-law of Edward Steichen, who lived near me in Connecticut and whom I sometimes met on train trips to New York. Steichen owned a large farm in Redding chiefly devoted to breeding delphiniums and other flowers, a pursuit he began in France in 1910. First a painter, he became a pioneer in the early development of photography as a fine art and a disciple of Alfred Stieglitz. He was born in Luxembourg, son of a copper miner and a milliner, and moved to rural Michigan as a child. In the First World War he was a technical adviser on aerial photography with the rank of colonel. He became photo-editor of various chic magazines and later the creator of the famous Museum of Modern Art exhibition "The Family of Man."

MODERN BUILDING

ITS NATURE, PROBLEMS, AND FORMS

BY WALTER CURT BEHRENDT

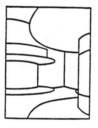

HARCOURT, BRACE AND COMPANY, NEW YORK

Decoration adapted from a photograph

A practical and worldly man, Steichen extended his work to include commercial portraiture and advertising. When I knew him he had a lucrative contract with the J. Walter Thompson advertising agency. Brilliant younger photographers were competing with him, and to impress the agency's clients it was arranged for Sandburg to write a short biography to be published by Harcourt, Brace, the costs underwritten by the agency. This was a rare procedure among established publishers, but the reputations of the two men made it acceptable. In 1929 I produced a large, elegant book, over fifteen inches tall, with Sandburg's text and about fifty photographs beautifully reproduced by Hugo Knudsen.

A few years before I knew Steichen, my friend Emanuel Benson, then a free-lance art critic, took me to see Alfred Stieglitz. An American Place, Stieglitz's art gallery, was publishing Benson's book about the painter John Marin, and Benson wanted me to design it. This led to my taking over all design and printing for the gallery. Stieglitz, born in 1864, had been the leader before the end of the nineteenth century in establishing photography as a fine art, and he is still considered to be one of America's greatest camera geniuses.

An American Place was devoted to showing photography and also to promoting the work of a small group of American painters which included Stieglitz's wife Georgia O'Keeffe, John Marin, Arthur Dove, and Marsden Hartley. These and many other painters and photographers constantly dropped in at the gallery, sometimes to do business with Stieglitz but usually for an exchange of art news and gossip. I was often there. Much earlier Stieglitz had pioneered in introducing European artists to an American audience. In 1911, at a gallery called 291, he showed twenty Cézanne watercolors, the first American exhibition of Cézanne's work.

Stieglitz hated being called an art dealer, but in fact he was one. He was an adroit showman and not quite as pure and indifferent to money as he liked people to think, and perhaps as he himself believed. He felt he was uniquely equipped to bring cultural enlightenment to the world. Confident of his mission, he demanded that his followers accept his ideas and prejudices. He later withdrew his friendship from Emanuel Benson because he did not approve of Benson's deprecating review of a highly laudatory book about him.

Stieglitz was for many years a patron and friend of Steichen, but by the time I knew him he was scornful of what he saw as Steichen's selling out for fame and material gain. None of Steichen's productive activity could atone for his going beyond the limits Stieg-

Modern
British Poetry

MID-CENTURY EDITION

EDITED BY LOUIS UNTERMEYER

HARCOURT, BRACE AND COMPANY · NEW YORK

Calligraphy by myself, type and layout to suit the illustration

litz set for true creative expression, and he criticized him without restraint both as artist and man.

In spite of being autocratic and quite in awe of his own ideals, Stieglitz was a stimulating influence on people he chose to include within his orbit, and for several years I was one of them. He en-

ARCHITECTURE
for the NEW THEATRE

EDITED BY EDITH J. R. ISAACS

THEATRE PLANNING, BY LEE SIMONSON
THEATRE TYPES, BY FREDERICK ARDEN
PAWLEY . . . A COMMUNITY THEATRE, BY
WILLIAM HOWARD LESCAZE . . . PROJECTS
BY NORMAN BEL GEDDES . . . NEW RUSSIAN
THEATRES . . MODERN SWEDISH THEATRES

Published for the National Theatre Conference

NEW YORK . . . THEATRE ARTS, INC. . . . 1935

Linecuts salvaged from magazine articles. Ignoring the customary margins produced pages that reflect the innovative use of space by theater builders.

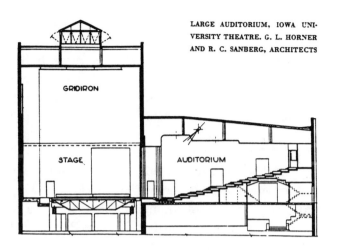

LARGE AUDITORIUM, IOWA UNI-
VERSITY THEATRE. G. L. HORNER
AND R. C. SANBERG, ARCHITECTS

GRIDIRON

STAGE

AUDITORIUM

PROJECT FOR A TEACHERS' COLLEGE

MOST theatres that are a part of a school building, even
those where much money is spent, lack good sightlines,
have poor acoustics, back-stages much too small, and
stage-houses too low for efficient lighting and scene
handling. These faults develop because the school architect crowds the theatre into whatever space is left after
classrooms, etc., have all been provided. Miss Effie
Georgine Kuhn approaches logically the problem of planning a theatre for the Drama and Music Department of
New Jersey State Teachers' College by first isolating
adequate space for auditorium and high stage-house and
then placing all necessary class and study rooms.

[69]

couraged my taste for a straightforward typographic style, and I have always been grateful for that.

Because of how they were organized and managed, the Harcourt, Brace publishing house and the Stieglitz art gallery seemed at opposite ends of the range of institutions I served. In the final analysis, however, their roles were not so different: they both brought the work of creators, be they writers or painters, to the people of the world. I was fortunate to have a part in expediting that process.

At this time I began a practice that I was to repeat for the rest of my life. I was not satisfied just to do my own job; I wanted to change, or at least to improve, everybody else's work and the conditions under which they functioned. At first I was concerned with the technical and artistic levels of the whole world of printing and publishing. Later I seemed to have the same missionary spirit about every field into which I moved.

I became active in organizations devoted to advancing the craft of bookmaking through discussions and exhibitions. I carried on a one-man campaign against the use of thick, soft papers, used by Knopf and a few others to increase the bulk and reduce the weight of books but poorly suited to take sharp impressions from type. I wrote about book design for *Publishers Weekly* and other periodicals. In the *Bookman*, a magazine of literary criticism, I had a monthly department for reviewing books on art, architecture, design, and other extraliterary subjects. My first essay appealing for a modern style was published in 1927 in Edwin Valentine Mitchell's *Book Notes*.

About 1931 I decided to organize a class in book design. My friend Fred Melcher, editor of *Publishers Weekly* and a strong voice in the industry for better bookmaking, helped me to set up my class in his office. Later I held it in my own new and larger studio on 26th Street. Then, three years after turning me down because I lacked academic credentials, Helmut Lehmann-Haupt asked me to relocate to the School of Library Service at Columbia University. After two years there I moved again, this time to the headquarters of the Book and Magazine Guild where we were starting technical classes for those who worked in publishing.

Over fifteen years my class drew a total of several hundred men and women. Needless to say, I learned a good deal about my trade while teaching, and I developed an ability to communicate ideas. My course was not a series of lectures on art and theory but a practical approach to the problems of putting a book together. I covered thoroughly the various ways to arrange each element in a book, the text page, chapter heads, contents, footnotes, index, and so forth, as well as the selection of paper and binding material. It was not difficult to demonstrate that arranging these elements (making the layouts) required aesthetic as well as technical choices and that the design would thus grow naturally out of their structure.

I tried to make clear that a book is not just a collection of two-dimensional surfaces; it is also a three-dimensional object with a life in time. I showed nineteenth-century books with undistinguished typography but with good paper and cloth and good proportions that were still pleasant to hold and read.

I put a great deal of emphasis on the choice of a typeface suited to the author's style and subject and to the paper it will be printed on. In discussing the design of typefaces, the most fundamental understanding the typographer must have, I looked for a way of explaining an artist's "hand," the unique personal impress that establishes the style and character of the letter and the whole alphabet.

I hit on a successful device: I passed around a pad of paper and one plain thick crayon and asked each student to draw a straight line. When these were compared, the surprising variation in these simple marks showed clearly the differences in the students' personalities and how the special character of each person's "hand" would determine the style of any drawing, painting, or type design that he or she might create.

An intimate acquaintance with type design and typefaces has been to me a lifelong source of pleasure. All literate persons are exposed constantly to the printed word, willingly in their reading and, whether or not they choose, in an environment saturated with signs and advertising. One of the failures of our education process is that students are almost never offered the basic knowledge that would equip them to appreciate the forms of the letters they see every day.

I am tempted to list typefaces that I like and have used, but there

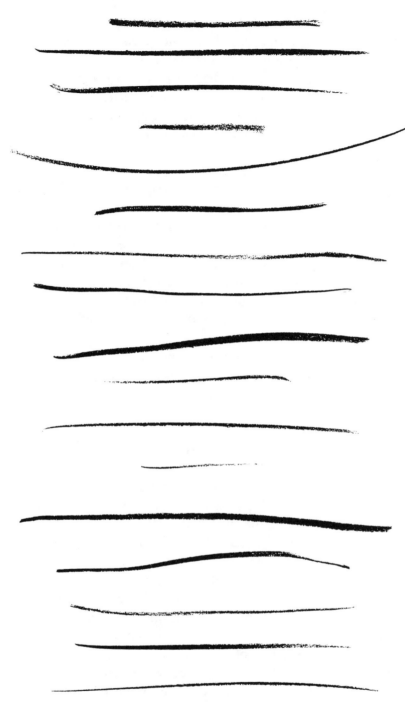

Crayon marks made by design students

are many versions of even a single type design and many mechanical ways of producing a readable page. The latest of these technologies is photocomposition, done by the computer for photoreproduction, with no metal type. This of course has had an enormous influence on type design. To treat this huge subject adequately is beyond the scope of this book.

When I started to work as a free lance at the end of 1925, there were new publishing houses providing opportunities for me. There was also a growing interest in improving the looks and structure of books. In New York, the American Institute of Graphic Arts was the leader in this movement. Typographers, printers, binders, museum and advertising people, and book collectors joined to hold discussions and exhibitions. I took part in this stimulating activity.

The Institute's competitive exhibition called Fifty Books of the Year got wide public notice, and by 1941 thirty-six of my books had won places in these shows, more than by any other designer. My work was also included in other group shows, and in 1941 I had a large one-man exhibition at the Book and Magazine Guild selected by Monroe Wheeler of the Museum of Modern Art.

By the mid-thirties, in spite of the effect of the Great Depression on the publishing industry, a few young designers were bringing modern concepts to books. Among these were Ernst Reichl, Paul Rand, John Begg, Alvin Lustig, Abe Lerner, Evelyn Harter, and Harry Ford. Joseph Blumenthal was not designing for mass production, but his Spiral Press had left the fussy decorated books of the other "fine printers" behind and was setting a new standard for clean, straightforward typography. The Institute sponsored a series of luncheon meetings which we called the Book Clinic, where designers, printers, and editors met to dissect contemporary books. Later we held informal exhibitions of trade books and textbooks.

While a few designers of type, mostly Europeans, had new ideas, most of the faces available were based on sixteenth-, seventeenth-, and eighteenth-century printing styles. The belief that handwork was always superior to machine work was slow to die. The hand-operated printing press was the icon of many a booklover, and happy was the designer who had one in his garage and could turn his back on sordid commercialism at five o'clock and hurry home to worship.

Report TO THE HONORABLE

LEGISLATURE OF THE STATE OF NEW YORK

OF THE JOINT LEGISLATIVE COMMITTEE TO

EXAMINE INTO, INVESTIGATE AND STUDY THE

EXISTING FACILITIES FOR THE CARE AND

TREATMENT OF CHILDREN now coming under the

Jurisdiction of the Children's Courts, and of Minors 16 to

18 years of age now coming under the Jurisdiction of the

Adult Courts, and of the advisability of changes in the

present method of handling cases of Minors 16 to 18

years of age, either by extension of the Jurisdiction of the

Children's Courts or by some other method.

Albany, New York   **April, 1942**

A document, not a reading book—the effort was to avoid its looking dull

The efficiency and economy of new technologies could not be ignored, however. In the nineteenth century the reproduction of photographs required smooth, clay-coated paper. With twentieth-century offset lithography, letters and pictures are transferred from an engraved plate to a rubber-covered roller and from that in turn

An Act TO REPEAL SUBDIVISION (D) OF SEC-
TION EIGHTY-THREE OF THE DOMESTIC RELATIONS COURT
ACT OF THE CITY OF NEW YORK, RELATING TO IMPOSITION
OF FINES, AND RENUMBERING CERTAIN SUBDIVISIONS OF
SUCH SECTION

*The People of the State of New York,
represented in Senate and Assembly, do enact as follows:*

Section 1. Subdivision (d) of section eighty-three of chapter
four hundred and eighty-two of the laws of nineteen hundred
thirty-three, entitled "An act to establish in and for the city of
New York a court of domestic relations, to be known as the
domestic relations court of the city of New York, and defining
its powers, jurisdiction and procedure and providing for its organization," as amended by chapter nine hundred and forty-three of
the laws of nineteen hundred forty-one, is hereby repealed.

§ 2. Subdivisions (e), (f), (g) and (h) of such section, as
amended by chapter nine hundred and forty-three of the laws of
nineteen hundred forty-one, are hereby renumbered, respectively,
subdivisions (d), (e), (f) and (g).

§ 3. This act shall take effect immediately.

EXPLANATION: Matter in *italics* is new; matter in brackets [ ] is old
law to be omitted.

 The State-wide Children's Court Act empowers the
judge of any children's court to visit any institution to
which a child may be remanded or committed by the
Children's Court of his County (section 45). The same
permission is also found in the Onondaga County Act
(section 2).

The New York City Court Act provides that each institution to which a child has been committed must be

51

to the paper. Each of these new processes gave the printed page a
look different from that produced by pressing metal type onto the
paper's surface. These technical changes presented new and difficult problems to the typographer, problems that were not simply
aesthetic or philosophical.

A conventional hands-off-the-author layout

It was perhaps the rigors of handling these technical changes that impelled some designers to use calligraphy and hand lettering to somewhat humanize their layouts. When I think of calligraphy I like to remember a writing master of the early seventeenth century whom a certain Mr. Bickham, in his book *Penmanship in Its Utmost Beauty and Extent*, referred to as "that celebrated Italian, Signor Lucas Materot, whose genius led him to the sole practice of the Italian hand, which he executed after so exceedingly neat and beautiful a manner that he flourished without a rival, was the admiration of all his contemporary Professors, and the Darling of the Ladies."

In 1980 the Grolier Club in New York held an exhibition of trade books published between 1920 and 1950. Charles Farrell, reviewing it in *Fine Print* magazine, said in part: "For several of the designers whose work was included, the selection can only be described as eccentric. The most important, Robert Josephy, was represented by four books, all excellent (I have never seen but one poor Josephy design and that was beginner's work from the mid-1920's). . . . Josephy was the single most important figure in American trade book design during the crucial decade 1930–40—much more important, for instance, than Dwiggins. He was the first professional free-lance book designer, and was one of the greatest designers in the history of American typography. His style—simple, clean-cut, and tasteful—was the antithesis of the essentially baroque typography emanating from Knopf. Although he is most often thought of as belonging to Harcourt, Brace—where he established his good taste with such force that it survived for some twenty years—he also worked for many other publishers. He is generally overlooked today because, first, he was working during the years of the Great Depression and therefore made no fancy books (i.e., collectors' toys), and second, because his style, though as personal as that of any other fine designer, was wholly free from idiosyncrasy and affectation; as a result he has never attracted any cult following."

Of course I knew that everyone did not agree with Farrell's comments. They came many years after I had reduced my typographic efforts to designing miscellaneous pieces of printing for nonprofit organizations, but nevertheless I was gratified to find that my hard work, forty and more years before, was not entirely forgotten.

I worked as a free-lance designer well into the 1950s. In 1934 I bought a farm to supplement my income and have a part-time country home. When I did so I did not anticipate that I would spend fifty years in agriculture. I did not give up working for publishers abruptly and did not decide until twenty years later that I was ready to quit that work. During those twenty years when I was both book designer and farmer, I did not lose my interest in typography, and I needed the income from designing while the farm was developing into a profitable enterprise. That does not happen quickly if a farm is devoted entirely to growing apples, pears, and peaches, but by 1955 the farm had become my chief source of income.

Meanwhile, the book publishing industry and my work for it were changing. I continued to produce trade books, technical and educational books, and books for university presses and others. School and college texts, at one time dull and homely, were providing new and interesting problems. Much of this development was due to efforts by me and a few colleagues to show how imaginative design could make these books better teaching tools, in addition to making more money for publishers. I worked on many of these, especially for Harcourt, Brace, during the last years I served as their designer.

On the whole, although I continued to find the practice of my trade rewarding, I was beginning to think I had done enough. I had produced literally thousands of books over thirty years and done my share of agitating for better design standards. There had always been printers who produced beautiful books by hand on a small scale, but their work had little influence on mass production in large plants. I had a part in demonstrating that the size of a shop did not determine the quality of its work.

A critic of the idea that only handwork could produce beautiful things once wrote: "Whatever the concepts machine, machine age, mechanistic, may stand for in most minds, we can be certain of only one thing; that they imply nothing that is not also present in fact or in principle in an ordinary hammer, a hand-thrown bobbin, a foot-power potter's wheel, or the simplest bellows forge. These are all tools. . . . As each grows more complex, it may get larger, work faster, produce more, but it does not of itself make either better or inferior goods unless geared that way. To use a machine, itself a fine thing, with skill and understanding is a matter of character." That is the sermon some of us tried to preach, and for a while people seemed to be listening.

When I started in the business in 1920 the person in the publishing office who produced the books was called the manufacturing man (there were no women in such jobs!). Creative talent was not required. The idea that he should be responsible for good design as well as for technical specifications grew out of efforts, in which I took part, to establish the concept and title of book designer. A few publishers, notably my former boss Alfred

Knopf, helped to demonstrate that good design and good materials were good business. By the 1950s it was taken for granted that attention to design was a proper and central part of the publishing process.

By the 1960s small new publishing houses, started by young men I had known in the twenties, were already growing into enormous conglomerates or had sold their names and lists of authors to these megapublishers. Older firms, founded in the nineteenth century, were being swallowed up. Whether this has been good for authors depends on what kind of books they write and on the market for their work. Whether it has been good for literature only history can decide. Whether it has been good for the craft of bookmaking I have earned the right to judge, and my verdict is that it has not.

It has long been the custom for publishing executives to be private and largely anonymous figures. In recent years money and power have brought some of them personal publicity. Along with this has come the implication that they are the chief creative people in the publishing process. In this lofty role they are too often removed from the details of how their books are made. They have permitted the design of trade books to become pretentious and tasteless, left to people trained as designers of advertising, people who have obviously never dealt directly with printers or even visited their shops. The subtleties of letter design have largely disappeared. I wish I could say that this decline in taste has cut their profits, but it apparently has not.

Most of these big changes in publishing, and in the physical quality of its product, occurred after my time. Friends have sometimes credited me with wisdom and foresight for quitting when I did, but few of those changes were visible in the 1950s. When I left the field I thought we had established standards that would survive. Even these gains, however, were chiefly within the narrow circles of printing and publishing. We were never able to reach a broad public. Appreciation of beautiful type and printing and binding has never been widely accepted as an essential part of a good education, a cultural resource bringing pleasure and enrichment to readers. This is the outstanding failure of our movement.

As for me, although I gave up working for commercial book publishers, I have never lost my interest in typography and printing. I continued to write and talk about design for some years, as a sort of emeritus member of the fraternity, and to design an occasional piece of printing. In the 1990s the publications of the Connecticut Agricultural Experiment Station in New Haven give me a chance to practice my old trade, and I enjoy that.

6 🍎 New Scenes, New Faces

Many stories have been written about life in American cities in the 1920s, and few of them are exaggerated. World War I was over, and people believed there could never be another one. The political consequences of the peace terms imposed on Germany were not yet visible. The collapse of the financial structure in late 1929 and the catastrophic economic depression it triggered came soon enough, but the decade that preceded it was a time of both expanded interest in the arts and of widespread patronage of public entertainment.

I was not only a very serious young man devoted to good books and good works, but I was just as serious about my pleasures, enjoying dates and parties, theaters, museums, art galleries, and nightclubs. Some of my friends could only be called frivolous.

When my family moved back to our Manhattan house in 1924, many of my friends were part of the entrenched upper-middle-class Jewish circle with which my parents were identified. Some of these families had become wealthy, but I cannot accuse them of snobbery, even though the parties and weddings they held for their daughters were elaborate and sometimes extravagant. Thinking about the significance of these peoples' way of living, I was beginning to feel uncomfortable among them, though I was still willing to accept their invitations.

Among my friends were two daughters of Arthur Lehman. His

85

brother, Herbert, had left the family bank to become a famous liberal Democratic governor and senator, but Arthur stayed with the bank. All I remember of him is his asking us, "Have you boys seen the building I gave to Harvard?" The Lehmans had a large "cottage" in the Lewisohn family compound at Upper Saranac Lake in the Adirondacks. Adolf Lewisohn was Mrs. Lehman's father, a retired copper baron. My sister Marian and I were invited for a week there. It was a most elegant camp; suburban living in an artfully devised rustic environment. Our daily pleasures were rigidly scheduled, a bit like the routine in a minimum security correctional facility. Every evening we were required to gather in the recreation hall to hear Mr. Lewisohn sing. He had taken up music late in life, had retained a personal teacher, and required an audience. A couple of his sons-in-law read their newspapers there, but we young people had to be on our good behavior.

Marian and I enjoyed other features of life at the camp, but reciprocating on the Lehman level was of course impossible for us. We did have one big party for Marian on 77th Street. It was too big for the house but still not too big for our family budget, and it seemed as if our friends enjoyed themselves as much as at some of the fancy "coming out" parties in downtown hotels. Sartorial perfection was required of fastidious young men at this time. The usual black tie tuxedo was not elegant enough; the "dress suit"— white tie, boiled shirt, and tailcoat—was the thing. This produced laundry bills which few young men could afford.

At that time I was convinced that carnal approaches to young women were not at all welcome—a mistake for which I have often berated myself. I spent much of my time with resolute virgins waiting to exchange their favors for wedding rings. Some of them enjoyed being kissed; some would not even go that far.

For some years my chief emotional outlet was dancing. I developed exceptional skill at the fast-moving ballroom steps popular at the time; sharing rapid movement with a responsive female was a powerful experience. I usually enjoyed this with a partner of whom I asked only expert collaboration and no other intimacy. Often she was expressing in dance sexual feelings that were otherwise carefully suppressed.

There were lots of opportunities for dancing. I went to private parties, some of them in other cities. I belonged to the Pall Mall Club, managed by the wife of my friend Stuart Rose, a sister of

Humphrey Bogart, which held weekly dances for young people in a hotel, and there were dances at colleges where my friends were preparing to face the realities of life.

A group of college students got the idea of holding semipublic dances during vacation periods to earn money. They hired the best dance bands to provide the music and hardened bouncers to maintain order. These affairs—called Intercollegiate Hops—attracted hordes of young people.

I remember one hop held at the famous but then bankrupt and vacant Delmonico's. Patrons, once admitted, were required to remain, to prevent ticket-swapping and other corruptions. A bouncer guarded the door, proclaiming loudly, "You can't return back, folks," and he meant it. On that evening a group of us, leaving for some reason and unable to "return back," set up a rump party with a portable Victrola on the sidewalk outside the hall.

Prohibition, a national law against the sale of alcohol, had been on the books since 1920, and the machinery for avoiding it was well established. Everyone had their favorite bootlegger or knew a source of grain alcohol to mix with the flavors sold at all drugstores. For a while I had a friend named Giles Healy who managed a chemical laboratory and could supply me with a safe and superior product. Under peer pressure I acquired a taste for liquor and have enjoyed it all my life. Except for a few occasions when I was quite young, I have been a moderate drinker, but I always look forward to that one stiff whiskey at the end of the day.

I spent a fair amount of time and money in nightclubs and cafés with good dance orchestras, sometimes good entertainment, and always set-ups for one's liquor. The pocket flask was standard equipment. Some of the best in show business performed at these clubs, especially the comedians. I thought Jimmie Durante, working with his stooges Clayton and Jackson, was the funniest man in the world. He dreamed up complicated acts which were a lampoon of current popular ideas. One, called "Wood," made fun of city people pretending to love nature and ended up with a huge pile of wooden objects and scrap wood which had been hidden about the premises. All this was accompanied, naturally, by appropriate music and lyrics.

There was in New York a generous supply of uniformly pretty small-town girls, completing their educations in the big city at chaperoned residences, who loved going to nightclubs. I think now that the pleasures of the dance somewhat delayed my establishing more intimate ties with young women. I began, however, to realize that sexual relations were changing. The widely read books of Freud and Havelock Ellis and the greater availability of contraceptives were speeding acceptance of the positive value of erotic expression. Moving among new people as a free-lance worker and having a place of my own brought me many new and less conventional friends.

I became acquainted with several theater publicity agents, and with them I attended many play openings on passes, including a bawdy Mae West play in Brooklyn that was never permitted to open in Manhattan. I developed an enthusiasm for the ballet and enjoyed, at a distance, a crush on a beautiful ballerina with American Indian blood named Maria Tallchief. For some reason I never had much interest in music and learned nothing about it. Except for an occasional concert, it has never been a part of my life.

Designing printing for museums and art galleries gave me an inside look at what artists were trying to do. I had ties, of course, with some of the writers whose books I was working on, but I gravitated naturally toward young painters and sculptors, and they became my friends. Some of them eventually were among the most widely known and admired American artists.

I felt I was receiving a pretty good education, better than I would have gotten at college, though obviously not in the same areas of knowledge and experience. When I made comparisons with what some of my friends were learning and examined my own temperament and habits, I was comfortable with my decision to go to work. I was aware that four more years of study and contemplation might have led me to some other field of work, and later in life I occasionally wished I had become an architect or a scientist, but on the whole I was happy with what I was doing.

Occasionally someone would call me an intellectual, a term I have always detested. Many people working in the arts, especially writers, seem to be delighted to classify their peers—and themselves by association—as intellectuals. Theirs is an assumption of superior intelligence and perception, even a capacity for elevated political judgment. The commercial and cultural apparatus that promotes and sells their work, that makes their names known, helps to establish public belief in their cerebral power. When I was older and spending much time with scientists, really educated people working in many disciplines, I found that they did not think of themselves as intellectuals. That confirmed my long-held belief that the term was fatuous and essentially without real meaning.

I lived on West 51st Street for two years. Hardwick Moseley, a traveling book salesman for Dutton's, shared the place with me during his short stays in New York. He was a delightful, warm, and humorous extrovert from Kentucky who saw me through my first marriage and much later started me on my second. In return I tried to talk him out of marrying a beautiful Massachusetts girl named Betty Proctor because he had known her for only two weeks. He ignored me and stayed with Betty until the end of his life. I, who entered marriage with much more caution, did not do that well.

Hardwick had a keen intelligence, masked by a "good old boy" Southern charm. He became an editor and sales director at the Houghton Mifflin Company and spent most of his years with them in Chicago and Boston. This leaves me with too few anecdotes to tell about our long close friendship but with unlimited affection and intimacy to remember. It was through Hardwick and Betty that I got to know Martha Davenport, my second wife. The four of us shared those warm feelings for the rest of our lives.

Among our neighbors was a group of young theater press agents, including the agreeable but exceedingly homely Lillian Hellman. We might have predicted that she would become a successful playwright but surely not that she would strive all her life to promote the fiction that she was a great femme fatale. Her husband, Arthur Kober, was a firmly urban fellow who leapfrogged from the streets of New York to the streets of Hollywood. When I saw him many years later he asked me a question I remember with pleasure. "What are you doing now, Bob?" "Farming," I told him, and he asked, "But Bob, do you *mind* living in the country?"

One of our diversions was shooting craps, which proved quite profitable for Hardwick and me. I found that the game was for me a psychological exercise, that you could frequently perceive when your opponent was losing confidence and was at your mercy. That talent did not addict me to lifelong gambling, but it paid off at the time.

Soon after I had my own living quarters. Following a few standard romantic experiments came my first serious emotional involvement, and one of my more painful ones. The woman was married to a conventional and jealous man to whom she was occasionally unfaithful. Our mutual attraction was overwhelming. Our first congress, at my studio, was not conducted efficiently. My friend, terrified of possible pregnancy and in an effort to conceal her infidelity, proceeded deliberately to become pregnant by her husband. Then she had an abortion, and as the villain in the case I was subjected to her neurotic outbursts for weeks. The experience made me wonder whether, being a matter-of-fact and not highly emotional male, I was particularly vulnerable to this kind of female manipulation.

After this rough start the going was easier. Having escaped from the circles of husband-hunters, I graduated into the company of free and self-reliant women and proceeded to make up for lost time. For a while I had an unusual set of principles guiding my efforts. Scornful of the standard laying-on-of-hands technique, I depended on philosophical argument, on the woman's responsibility for making bold and independent decisions about her own life. I did not find this approach at all successful.

In 1925 I met Harold Ross. He had an idea for a new magazine, and someone told him I could help him get it into production. He had little money; we planned an inexpensive black-and-white job, with line drawings for which I looked up some of my artist friends. Fortunately for him, Ross acquired a wealthy backer before anything was printed, and the first issue of the *New Yorker* was published in the style which it has kept, with practically no changes, for over sixty years. Ross had no further need for my help, and I never saw him again.

Among my other friends at the time was Catherine Bauer, a Vassar graduate working in book advertising at Harcourt, Brace. I was asked to coach her in the selection and use of types, and that led to a rewarding relationship. I remember especially that we shared a deep interest in architecture and laughed a great deal about almost everything. She had an early concern for public housing problems, and this attracted her to my friend Lewis Mumford, with whom she was later intimate for many years. She served as a sort of sounding board for Mumford's ideas. He saved copies of his quite didactic letters to her, and they appear as a major part of his autobiographical *My Work and Days*.

I have often thought of Catherine's talent for laughter and wondered how that fitted with Lewis's total lack of any sense of humor.

That was evident when I knew him as a young man and is apparent in his writings and in his fine biography by Donald Miller. I had been an admirer and friend of Mumford since reading his early *Sticks and Stones*, and I designed many of his books at Harcourt, Brace. We were friends for ten or fifteen years but parted in 1939 after a bitter political argument about the Nazi-Soviet pact.

I had an illustrator friend named Harry Morse Myers. One day he asked me to pose for him for a magazine cover drawing. He said his model had stood him up, though I suspected that he had no cash to pay a model. I found that I was to stand embracing a show-girl named Peggy Fish. Needless to say, she was very handsome, and physical contact with her started a friendship. She was observant, humorous, and quite casual about sex. I remember her saying she wanted to believe in reincarnation but was troubled that one always seemed to come back to earth as a bunch of grapes.

In those days homosexuals kept their inclinations secret, and this sometimes led to surprises. I made the acquaintance at a party of an agreeable young writer and invited him to my place for conversation. He made an unexpected sexual proposal which I rejected righteously and scornfully. It was my first and only such experience. Many years passed before even the most tolerant of people began to understand sexual preferences and to recognize the rights and dignity of people emotionally different from themselves.

One of my longest friendships was with Emanuel Benson. I knew him first as a writer and free-lance art critic. I was impressed with his erudition and found that we shared many tastes and perceptions, as well as views of the world beyond art. When he became a curator at the Philadelphia Museum I designed many pieces of printing for that institution. I was at the hospital to comfort him when his emotionally unstable first wife nearly lost her mind during childbirth. His second and very happy marriage, to a colleague at the museum named Elaine Goff, was celebrated at our house in Bethel. They left Philadelphia and opened the Benson Gallery in Bridgehampton, which became the most successful and influential center for art on eastern Long Island. Emanuel was stricken with cancer in 1971 and was the first of my close friends to die. It was through Benson that I met Alfred Stieglitz.

I got to know Edward Norman when he was still at Harvard. He was my only friend from a wealthy family who had any sort of serious social conscience. His father had left Chicago and a partnership in Sears Roebuck to become an independent financier; increasing his fortune was his vocation. Edward wanted no part of this. He was involved in the Consumers' Cooperative movement, which in the twenties had hopes of reforming the whole economic system.

Ed was a charming and impulsive extrovert. His attachment to a wide-eyed, solemn, rather humorless Philadelphia friend of mine named Dorothy Stecker came on the rebound from his longtime pursuit of a frivolous debutante. They were soon married and, following Dorothy's taste, lived in a Park Avenue apartment furnished with expensive rustic simplicity. I was a frequent visitor there and also at their Cape Cod summer place at Woods Hole. Ed's father was constantly pressing him to give up his nonpaying activities and participate in fortune building, and he finally yielded. As far as I could see, and I was very close to them at that time, Dorothy made only weak efforts to help Ed keep his independence. One result was that more funds became available to finance Dorothy's ambitious cultural activities.

Dorothy met Alfred Stieglitz in 1926 when she was twenty-one and he was sixty-two. She was soon participating in the management and financing of An American Place. Fascinated with Alfred, Dorothy developed an intense spiritual-intellectual-romantic relationship with him. She began to treat Edward as beneath her intellectual level. In his presence and mine, she would make long, intimate phone calls from Woods Hole to Stieglitz at Lake George. The implied comparison was devastating to Edward's ego, though she seemed comfortable believing her actions were justified by her high ideals. It is clear in her memoirs, published in 1987, that Dorothy could not perceive, or would not face, the effects of her behavior either on Edward or on Alfred's marriage to Georgia O'Keeffe. I barely knew O'Keeffe, but the impact on her is fully described by her biographers.

My friendship with Edward continued; in 1934 he loaned me money to help me pay for the Bethel farm. By then I had been married for several years. Despite my long and close association with her husband, Dorothy was not above snubbing my new wife because Jane somehow did not meet her intellectual standards. That finally ended my intimacy with the Normans. Edward and Dorothy were divorced in 1946, leaving her a very wealthy woman. She was able to underwrite the publication of her writings, support favorite cultural enterprises, entertain celebrated people, and to dabble in Hindu religion and politics. Edward, married again to a woman very different from Dorothy, died at middle age.

One of my closest and longest friendships was with Alexander Calder. Sandy came to the Knopf office in 1924 to show me some sketches of animals because ours was the publishing office nearest the zoo, where he had made the sketches. Next time I saw him he had returned from four years in Paris determined to make his way in New York art circles.

By then I had become attracted to Beekman Place, a short street with houses overlooking the East River. It had not yet become chic, and I had another inexpensive top floor apartment there with, believe it or not, my own sheet-iron garage in the yard. Calder stayed there with me for a while, made some new acts for his miniature puppet circus, and prepared for his first big sculpture exhibition. His behavior was an amiable mixture of innocence and calculation, with a rather primitive approach to personal relations. A few young women complained to me about his sudden lunging advances.

Sandy was a big man who took up a lot of space in my little flat. Often when I came home from some job I would find that he had expanded his work area and contracted mine. A few days after his arrival he said I was about to meet a young pianist with a marvelous shape who had crossed from Europe with him. Her name was Louisa James, and she was indeed marvelous in many ways. I think she was Sandy's first serious love, and she turned out to be the perfect wife and partner. Her grandfather was one of two James brothers who, she always insisted, learned to drink in the Union Army and never amounted to much. The other James brothers, Henry and William, were too young to fight and escaped that corruption.

Sandy soon had his first New York exhibition of wood and wire sculpture. Eventually these evolved into the mobiles and stabiles which made him famous. He also produced paintings and a quantity of wire and tin and wood artifacts which could be seen in all his friends' kitchens. His circus had a cast of puppet caricatures of circus people and animals, about one-twelfth life-size. They were made to do a variety of ingenious stunts accompanied by Sandy's verbal encouragement of the action and by music on Louisa's gramophone. Most people loved the circus, but there was one exception. Aline Bernstein, a Theatre Guild stage designer, asked Sandy to give a show at her apartment. She thought it was to be a private performance and was unprepared when Sandy brought along a crowd of friends, including my wife and me. Thomas Wolfe, her lover at the time, was there. Reflecting her dismay, he wrote a sneering account of Sandy and the circus in his next novel, *You Can't Go Home Again*.

Sandy and I remained intimate friends for fifty years. In 1932 he and Louisa stopped in to see me in Weston, Connecticut. Sandy had no money with him and borrowed ten dollars which he used that day for a deposit on an old farmhouse in Roxbury. Two years later, when I was trying to buy a farm in Bethel, the Calders loaned me part of what I needed, much more than ten dollars.

Sandy's mother, Nanette, was a painter, and his father and grandfather were prominent sculptors, chiefly of large public monuments. His father, Sterling, and I became good friends. Sterling's own work, in the disciplined style of his time, was accurate, precise, and polished. Late in life he told me that he envied Sandy's free hand but knew he could not change his own way of working.

Louisa had some means, and Sandy's great success eventually made them very prosperous. They acquired houses and studios in France, where we visited them now and then. Later in life they were constantly surrounded by admirers, and it became an effort to see them. People like to toss the word genius around freely, but every detail of Sandy's work and personality deserved the term. He was the only true genius I ever knew.

Another friend was a very clever dress designer named Elizabeth Hawes, who was making a reputation among New York buyers of chic plumage. She had a modest salon for which Calder and I constructed furniture and decorations; a group of our friends often gathered there. Her current admirer was a sculptor named Ralph Jester. The three of us held a ball in Ralph's fifth-floor studio; the big feature was a real bathtub which we lugged up four flights of stairs to use for mixing the bootleg liquor. Acting out the common joke about bathtub gin was probably the most laborious stunt of the whole Prohibition era.

Ralph wanted to learn ceramics to use in his sculpture. He persuaded me to enroll with him in a pottery class at a Greenwich Village settlement house. He did not stay with it to the end, but I did. I found I very much enjoyed throwing pots and firing them in the kiln. I mixed an assortment of glazes of my favorite colors and took them to the farm, hoping to do some potting there, but I never had time to do it.

At that period I also became interested in uses for aluminum, which had recently become available in many forms of tubes, rods, and bars and which could be cut, bent, and hammered without heat. Money was scarce, and I tried designing lamps and other artifacts for sale. For a while a fancy Fifth Avenue store was selling my stuff, but soon large manufacturers began to use the metal, and I could not compete.

I did get an industrial designer friend named Russel Wright interested in aluminum, and much of his great success in designing stylish housewares came from using it. I myself used aluminum for many fixtures and devices in my own house later. Using it taught me new things about metalworking, and I made some brass and bronze hardware. Much as I wanted to be entirely self-sufficient, however, the needs of the farm soon diverted me to other kinds of construction.

The 1920s were exciting years for me. In a decade I grew from an eager kid just out of school to a seasoned technician working in a niche that I carved out for myself in the book publishing industry. Those years prepared me for my best work as a designer, which I did in the 1930s and the 1940s. They also convinced me that I should not depend entirely for my living on the income from making books.

I became acquainted with an assortment of people from varied backgrounds doing creative work in many fields. I was free to taste and enjoy the cultural experiences available to a single young man with his eyes and ears open and plenty of energy. Finally, at the end of the decade, I found myself a wife.

7 🍎 *A Marriage and a Farm*

Early in 1930 I went to meet Peggy Fish at a rehearsal of a musical play in which she had a small part. As I watched and listened, I was struck by the face and carriage of a very tall blond actress with a magnificent contralto voice. I met her some weeks later—I cannot recall where—and was immediately smitten.

Her name was Henrietta Enck, a name which exactly suited her personality, but she went under the stage name of Jane Alden, which did not. She had come from Texas, where she had been called the child wonder of the San Antonio Musical Club. Her youth was pleasant and uneventful. One of her few stories was about going to parties at a nearby army air base and meeting a flight instructor named Charles Lindbergh who was thoroughly disliked for playing practical jokes on timid air cadets. This taste was well known to the reporters who covered his exploits later but carefully omitted from their stories.

San Antonio was no metropolis. Jane's people were mostly German-Lutheran country preachers; her father was a wholesale grocer in the city. One of the notorious fluctuations in the sugar market left him in financial trouble. Her mother was eccentric, unrealistic, but energetic; she chaperoned her daughter to New York to recoup the family fortunes, confident of her triumph in show business. One sign of their naive ideas was attaching to Henrietta's unique personality the trite stage name of Jane Alden. Her real name was lost in the past long before I knew her.

Jane's talents did get her some parts in spite of her unusual height, but before she was really established in the theater she was lured into a brief marriage by a family-dominated playboy from Pittsburgh. When I met her she was twenty-six, back on Broadway, and slowly becoming known.

She was affectionate, sensitive, and humorous, as well as beautiful. I loved her height. It was a pleasure to stand embracing her and find her pretty face at the same level as mine. She was emotional where I thought I was not, and our backgrounds could not have been more different, but somehow our tastes and attitudes fitted together. She was happier in the country than in the city. I was not like anyone she had ever known, which apparently appealed to her. As for me, I thought that a freely emotional companion could complement my personality, as I perceived it. This was an error of judgment I was to repeat.

In the summer of 1930 we spent nearly every weekend with my friends the Dunnes in Westport. Finley Peter Dunne, Jr., worked for the *New York World*, the favorite newspaper of people like us but soon to be abandoned by its owner, Joseph Pulitzer, because it was losing money. Peter's friends included several ship news reporters. Their beats were important when newsworthy people traveled on steamships, and they brought us accounts, no doubt exaggerated, about romantic encounters with publicity-seeking actresses and other eager women they met on the job.

Peter's father was the creator of the marvelous widely syndicated Mr. Dooley monologues, observations on the world and its inhabitants by an Irish saloonkeeper. Sad to tell, Mr. Dunne's friend Payne Whitney thought that release from the daily newspaper grind would free him to do more serious writing. Whitney gave him half a million dollars, Mrs. Dunne bought a house in Southampton, and Mr. Dunne never wrote another line of any kind.

One weekend the Dunnes' friend Donald Freeman brought a fellow *Vanity Fair* staffer named Claire Booth Brokaw, recently divorced and not yet in pursuit of Henry Luce. They were there on an assignment to visit and write about the photographer Edward Steichen who lived nearby in Redding. We were all agreed that with her narrow bony face and lack of charm Donald's friend would not go very far; neither her writing skills nor her fierce ambition were yet in evidence.

I made a brass and copper weathervane for the Dunnes' roof. It was inspired by a medieval philosophical concept of which I was the author: "Angels don't care which way the wind blows." When the Dunnes moved to Hollywood it graced my garage roof in Bethel, and for fifty years it helped me decide when to spray my trees. One morning when I was asleep a hunter put two bullets through the angel's wings, but being immortal, it survived.

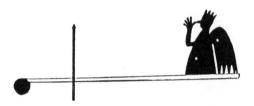

Prohibition had been the law of the land since 1920, and the drinking of alcohol had become almost obligatory. On one of our first dates I found out how this affected Jane. We were climbing the stairs to her apartment when she suddenly collapsed. She had not had much to drink, and I was astonished. I soon learned that even a little alcohol would depress and sicken her, could destroy her senses without giving her any pleasure or stimulation. That worried me, of course, but, with the confidence of youth, I was sure I was strong enough to help her. A few of my less diplomatic friends showed some doubts about the inevitability of our union, but everyone was extremely fond of her.

We were happy together, and by the fall of 1930 we had decided to marry. My mother, who had cautioned me against holding hands with a girlfriend when I was fifteen, telephoned us on our wedding day saying, "It's time for the bride and groom to get up." The world and my mother had moved, but I found presently that I still hadn't learned much about females. Jane was afraid that her previous divorce might not be valid in New York State so we were married in Englewood, New Jersey, by a police judge in knickers while his golf partners waited outside the courtroom. With us were my parents and an aunt of Jane's who was on the faculty of a nearby college.

The economy had improved very little since the 1929 panic; Roosevelt's efforts to "prime the pump" had taken many people

With Jane, 1931

off the breadlines, but they had raised hopes more than they raised wages. Jane and I proceeded to set up housekeeping on a scale not justified by the realities. Publishers were recovering slowly; my income was still down, and Jane wasn't having much luck in the theater, in spite of her looks and voice. There were few parts for a five-foot ten-inch woman; leading men were too short, and five-foot ingenues more appealing. She did have some parts in operettas, often as an unsympathetic haughty character. She had a naive idea of how to project herself and how to impress producers, and there was little anyone could do to help her.

We rented the basement and parlor floor of an old house on Beekman Place with a backyard overlooking the East River. It was a charming place which we could not afford. After two years we moved to 26th Street east of Fourth Avenue, nearer to publishing offices and at a rent nearer to what I could pay. My grandfather Spero, when I told him where it was, said, "Oh, there's a house of assignation on the corner." That was the Elton, a little fleabag hotel on Fourth Avenue. I doubt that Grandpa had ever had an assignation there, or anywhere else, but his office was nearby and he knew the gossip of the neighborhood.

In the mid-thirties I had a stay at St. Vincent's Hospital in New York. I went there for a hernia operation because Jane's surgeon-friend Gerald O'Brien was on the staff. It was my first inside view of a religious institution. The administrators were nuns; secure in the virtue of their heavenly vocation, they terrorized the nonunion lay nurses who worked under them. I established a bad reputation by reading the *Daily Worker* and other radical literature in bed. By the time I was well enough to exercise in the halls I had grown a beard and rather resembled the figure of Jesus which stood there. The nuns found this somewhat unsettling. At the time this amused me, but thinking back I am not so proud of flaunting my political and religious differences in such a place. I was not asked to feign piety, but I might have had more respect for the beliefs of those who had taken me in with no questions asked.

From our time in Westport came the idea of finding a place to pass the summers in Connecticut. We found one in the adjoining town of Weston and spent the warmer months of the next three years there. We were able to rent, for twenty-five dollars a month, a dilapidated but habitable house with only one leak in the roof, and that over the bathtub. The house was on a run-down farm which the owner hoped to sell to some big buyer. It had been owned by Steve Waterbury, the last of an old Weston family. Steve was a rare creature among farmers, a bachelor. He sold his livestock and moved to a small place up the road.

Nothing else had changed when I took over. There was a beautiful big barn with feed bins made of very wide pine boards and the usual other small buildings. There was a large side-hill orchard through which I never even walked and on the hilltop fields for corn, hay, and pasture. I was interested only in using the house and the vegetable garden, but I could not ignore the atmosphere of the whole place. Long before our three years ended I knew I would have to own a farm, and soon.

In 1929 I had an income of nearly $10,000 from design fees; in 1930 it was down to $6,000. Publishers, like everyone else, were in a panic, and my services were looked on as a luxury they could not at that time afford. It seemed to me, with no great confidence in the capitalist system, that I ought to be working at something that met the more basic needs of the human race, such as farming. This was a sensible conclusion, but I was in no position to act on it. I had not saved any money, and buying a farm would have to wait.

Meanwhile we were enjoying life in Weston. We swam in Long Island Sound at Westport. Jane appeared in the first production of the Westport Country Playhouse, singing between the acts of the play *Green Grow the Lilacs*, which later became the book of *Oklahoma*. I went regularly to New York to see publishers and printers, worked in our garden, and even acted the part of a ridiculous butler in an amateur murder play.

Weston was not as rural as it appeared to be. It had fine trees and many old houses, but by the thirties it had become, like Westport, to which it was a satellite town, the home of many commuters employed in New York advertising and related enterprises. One of our neighbors was John B. Watson, a psychologist who had made a reputation at Johns Hopkins University with a theory he called behaviorism and who then moved to the J. Walter Thompson advertising agency to apply his insights to marketing their clients' merchandise.

There was also a substantial population of theater people, writers, and artists in the two towns. Everett Shinn, who had once

The farmhouse, 1934 (left) and 1951

been a respected member of a group of innovative painters sometimes called the Ashcan School, was a good friend. Everett was
only in his late fifties, but his work and standing had declined,
chiefly it seemed to me because he was more interested in women
as companions than as models, but he was amiable and hospitable.

Another neighbor was Franklin P. Adams, editor of a popular
column in the *World* called the Conning Tower. Having a joke or
an anecdote or a bit of verse printed by him was a minor triumph,
and I was proud to make the Tower a few times. Lee Simonson,
the stage designer member of the Theater Guild group, was a frequent visitor. One day a rising literary critic named Van Wyck
Brooks came with him to visit us, riding in Lee's open car in a
formal suit topped by a derby hat.

The Great Depression was far from over, and many people who
could not accept Marxist theories of capitalist crisis were dreaming
utopian dreams. One of these ideas, called technocracy, advocated
tight control of all industrial resources and reorganization of the
entire social system under the leadership of engineers and technol-
ogists. My friend Charles Bonner, a public relations man, was for
a while an ardent technocrat. He tried hard to show me the perfec-
tions of a technocratic world.

Early in 1934 my Weston landlord found his buyer. I was unable

to find a similar place to rent, and I was forced to try to buy a farm without any money or give up the idea of living in the country. I was faced with a difficult decision, the first difficult one that I had ever had to make. Going to work at Knopf's had involved no long-term commitment, and I had no doubts about wanting to marry Jane.

Buying a farm was different. The land and the town and a new occupation presented a huge challenge. I was starting on a course that would be hard to reverse, whether or not I left my previous career and associations behind. The question was where to locate. I had already decided that Weston was not for me. I wanted to be in a town with an economic life of its own. The Fairfield County town of Bethel, twenty miles north, seemed to be such a place. There are towns named Bethel in many states. The name means House of God, and many pioneers adopted it, perhaps seeking forgiveness for sins against the Indians.

Real-estate agents did not believe that I could or would run a farm. They saw lots of customers who just wanted to play at being country people, but I finally found one who took me at my word. He sold me a run-down farm in Bethel with about fifty acres of what looked to me like good soil and a small shack of a house that kept the price down. It was on a gravel road, and there was still no electric power service in that part of town. I bought it for $7,500, financed by a mortgage and some cash borrowed from Ed Norman and the Calders. Our daughter Maria was born in October of 1933, and in the spring of 1934 the three of us were installed at the farm.

I had to decide then on what to grow and finally decided on fruit. There were about twenty-five old apple trees on the farm, trees past their prime which I soon cut down but which gave me the idea. Having to be away working on books, I could not undertake anything that would need daily care; that meant no livestock and no vegetables. I learned that I could start an orchard with very little knowledge and that it would not need much attention for the first years, so I planted my first orchard in the spring of 1935, and I was in business.

At that time Jane had a painful encounter with one aspect of Broadway life. She was hired by George White for his *Scandals* review and given major parts singing and acting in it. This was a promising opportunity; in the cast with her was Rudy Vallee, then a big name, vaudeville stars Willy and Eugene Howard, and still-to-be-famous Ethel Merman and Ray Bolger. In the chorus was a young woman named Alice Faye.

White was a diminutive, aggressive fellow known for his habit of preying on young chorus girls. He assumed that Jane's comradely manner was an invitation; when the show went to Atlantic City for a tryout he expected intimacies. When he found he had misjudged Jane he cut her parts ruthlessly, in spite of her key place in the production. This sounds like a standard show-business myth, but it actually did happen. What the incident drove home to me was that Jane had never developed the veneer of sophistication that would protect her from the hurts of one of the world's most brutal vocations.

She had plenty of talent. With her striking looks and voice, her height was no great handicap, but she never knew quite how to present herself. When she sang for a few friends she had a charming way of tapping out a few notes as she sat at the piano, but at a large party or an audition she would appear with an accompanist and stand before the piano like a diva, singing Tin Pan Alley songs in her glorious voice. I could never convince her that this stance was wrong for her, that it hid the very things that delighted people.

In 1935 Jane was "at liberty" as actors say, and she was persuaded by some Weston friends who had gone to work as screenwriters in Hollywood to try her luck there. The invention of sound was transforming the movie business and creating a wave of movies with music. With an introduction from Arthur Hopkins, an influential New York producer who admired her, she took our two-year-old daughter, picked up her mother in Texas, and drove to the West Coast. Her luck was no better there than in New York. She stayed long enough to become thoroughly discouraged and increasingly dependent on alcohol. She finally gave up her hopes for a movie career and came home to the farm, but she never really recovered from the experience and made little further effort to find jobs in the theater.

We were dividing our time between the farm and the Manhattan place on East 26th Street. In 1935 I became involved in the founding and leadership of the Book and Magazine Guild. There were many meetings, some at our apartment. I was holding my design class at 26th Street, and I was producing as many books as I could to pay our bills.

At the farm I had to prune and spray my new orchard even though the trees were too young to bear fruit. Some fields had to be harrowed, others mowed. I had a big vegetable garden and plenty of work to improve the house and farm buildings. Jane and Maria stayed there when the weather was good. Maria, whose name was always pronounced Mar-eye-a, in the old-fashioned way, and not Mar-ee-a, was a delightful, happy child, Jane a capable and always affectionate mother in spite of her distress about her career and her growing dependence on alcohol. For a while she was able to conceal her drinking from me; I first realized how far it had gone when some alert friends told me. Alcohol was for her a poison, not a stimulant. It brought her pain and no pleasure, but she could not break her addiction.

It gradually became clear to me and to our friends that our marriage was past saving. How much my many activities added to the stress I cannot say; certainly they were a factor. I no longer believed that my love and energy could keep Jane out of trouble, but I also knew that my obligations to my clients, the farm, and the

Guild were leaving her alone too much of the time. In 1937 Maria was approaching four, and I reasoned that the breakup of her family at that age would affect her less than it might when she was even a year or two older. Perhaps a wiser and more mature husband could have saved Jane, but I had lost all confidence in my ability to help her.

Early in 1937 Jane and I decided to separate. She moved to a small apartment near the Bank Street School, where Maria attended kindergarten. I found another in the series of top floor flats where I could roost when I came to the city to see publishers and tend to Guild business. I had a friend named Will Glass, a native of Albuquerque, New Mexico, who was employed by my old Danish friend Hugo Knudsen, an inventor and lithographic printing expert. Will knew and admired Jane, and when I told him that she was alone he went to see her promptly.

At first Jane had an idea that she wanted to have the farm; she said it was the only home she had ever had. I knew that was an illusion; her family was firmly established in San Antonio, and she was raised in a comfortable house there. She did go to the farm, her father came from Texas to help her, and with Will they kept things going after a fashion for one season. Her helpers finally persuaded her to give up the farm idea. She proceeded with our delayed divorce, and she and Will were married. Hugo Knudsen liked to say that water rusts the stomach; unfortunately, Will believed that too. He was a steady drinker, never visibly intoxicated or out of control but hardly the man to help Jane overcome her alcoholism.

When Maria was six she was accepted at the Hunter College Model School in an experimental program for future teachers attending Hunter. Our divorce agreement provided for shared custody of our child, but in reality Maria was with me at least two-thirds of the time. She spent all her weekends and vacations at the farm; now and then she went to my mother's house in Mt. Kisco.

It was wartime; two or three years after their marriage, Will went to France to serve as a lithographer in an army map-making unit, and without him Jane's illness was aggravated. The periods when Maria was staying with Jane were very difficult. Jane was often unable to function at all, and there were occasional crises that ended with her being hospitalized. Maria, at the age of seven or eight, was taking care of her. She did that remarkably well, with

With Maria, about 1939

only a little backup from me. Jane, with all her distress, never gave the child any reason to doubt her affection. Of course I was worried about her having such responsibility, but I was afraid that, if I cut all of Maria's ties to her mother, Jane would break down completely.

During those early years I was in some ways as dependent on Maria as she was on me. We often recall a typical Christmas. I had driven to New York on Christmas Eve to deliver a pickup truckload of mail-order gift packages of apples. Late in the evening Maria and I drove to the farm, lighted the stove, and went to bed. Next morning we went out to cut a wild cedar for our Christmas tree. The closeness of our relationship, fixed in those strenuous times, has never diminished. I regret to say that I was never able to duplicate it with my later children, who grew up under very different circumstances.

In 1944 Maria's sad period with Jane ended. The program at Hunter covered only five years, ending when Maria was nearing eleven, and she had to change schools. Without my needing to make an issue of Jane's health and competence, she agreed to Maria's going to boarding school. I wanted her to be at a school near Bethel so that I could see her often and sometimes take her home for weekends. We visited two nearby New York schools with elementary grades, the Manumet School in Pawling and Drew Seminary in Carmel. Manumet had an innovative progressive coed program; it was located on a former farm, and the children combined classes with outdoor work. Drew was an old-fashioned girl's school with big buildings and big trees and dignified big teachers in corsets. It was affiliated with the Methodist Church.

Manumet suited my theories about education, but when I asked Maria which school she preferred she said that Manumet was too much like home on the farm and Drew was like the schools she had read and thought about. I was dubious. The Drew headmaster seemed to be as proud of the dining hall as he was of the classrooms, but when I made some inquiries about him I learned that he had been a first-rate student at Princeton and had an excellent reputation as an educator. Meanwhile his daughter, who worked for a New York publisher, told him that she had heard of me and doubted that I would have any special interest in the dining hall. On our second visit the conversation was different, and Drew looked better.

Maria went to Drew for two years, the seventh and eighth grades. By the middle of the second year she decided that Drew was a bit stuffy (which it was), and she was ready for a less conventional school and one with less emphasis on religion. She went to the Putney School in Vermont, another progressive school on a farm but older and larger than Manumet, and with a reputation for brilliant teaching and successful graduates.

Maria saw very little of Jane during her two years at Drew, and in November of 1946, during Maria's second month at Putney, Jane died. She had developed cirrhosis, a disease of the liver frequently caused by alcoholism. Her death at forty-three, nine years after our separation, ended her years of constant illness and Maria's years of worry and responsibility.

The decision to leave Jane was the most painful I ever had to make. I was convinced, and my friends agreed, that I could not hope to end her addiction, but other questions remained: Should I stay with her indefinitely to help her where I could? What duties and restraints would Jane's condition impose on Maria as she grew up in this family of three? What effect would my retaining responsibility for Jane have on my work as a designer and in the Guild? Was I allowing Will Glass's presence to give me unreasonable confidence that Jane would be adequately cared for? If I had been religious, perhaps these questions would have been answered for me, but I could not seek that comfort.

My marriage to Martha, just before Jane's death, gave Maria a devoted second mother, and she grew up to have a stable and happy life. These events could not be foreseen, of course, and they do not answer my questions about the wisdom of my 1937 decision.

8 🍎 *In the Class Struggle*

When I left the security of my job at Knopf's late in
1925 to try my luck as a free lance, Europe was already being
shaken by the first aggression of Italian fascism. In 1929 the collapse of the American stock market and banks triggered a panic
(euphemistically called a depression) which was to last until World
War II. The Fascist rebellion against the democratically elected
government in Spain and the growing Fascist movements elsewhere in Europe were being supported by influential people, and
the United States, French, and British governments were giving
the democrats little support.

In America, citizens at every economic level and in every vocation were alarmed by the Fascists' oppression of workers and
the destruction of their institutions. Many looked to organized
labor to lead the opposition to fascism. Unions were forming in
industries where they had never before existed, attracting even
such self-employed individualists as writers and painters, who had
always prided themselves on being above politics. John O'Hara,
the novelist, once said to me, "I was sitting on the fence for a
long time, but then I realized that they were taking down the
fence."

One spring day in 1935 I encountered on a New York street an
Austrian-born book designer named Andor Braun. He asked me
whether I wanted to go to a meeting to discuss setting up some

kind of economic organization for workers in publishing. He was surprised to hear that I was very much interested, surprised because I had few close friends among publishing people and my social attitudes were not known. Some people saw me as a bit stuffy and a likely supporter of the status quo.

I thought of myself, however, as a convinced radical. I had in childhood seen the assumptions of privilege and superiority that grew out of the prosperity of a well-meaning family. I got a good view of the military mind at Bordentown. I had encountered the conflicting interests of employer and employee in my job at Knopf's. By the time I cast my first vote in 1924 for Bob La Follette, the Farmer-Labor candidate for president, the direction of my thinking and reading was fixed.

By 1935 Europe's struggles with fascism only confirmed and strengthened my conviction that what Marx called the contradictions of capitalism were destroying society. It was inevitable that I would welcome a chance to take part in the growing class conflict. Our first small meeting was the beginning of the Book and Magazine Guild, which we planned to model after the already flourishing Newspaper Guild. We would start as an educational association to develop in publishing employees a sharper understanding of where their economic and political interests lay. Collective bargaining might come later.

Publishing office jobs attracted educated young people; they liked the idea of being part of an enterprise associated with literature. They were willing to accept low pay for all jobs from beginning clerks to editors and technicians. The wages, starting at twelve dollars a week, were low even for depression years. In the course of my work for publishers I had come to know many people in many offices, and I welcomed the chance to help raise standards in the business where I made my living. I had not anticipated being part of an organization aimed at doing this, but once it was proposed, it seemed a natural step for me.

I had learned two things from William Morris. First, that good craftsmanship was closely related to the economic well-being of workers, and I agreed with that. Second, he found a conflict between his socialist theories and a changing technology, but I avoided that conflict by concentrating on mass production. I felt comfortable, therefore, in joining a movement consistent with my social ideas, and I was happy to align myself with people who did not accept the status quo, people with zeal for improving the world.

There was a great feeling of solidarity among Guild members, an exciting sense of mission and of opportunity. For me this was a new experience. I had exerted myself to improve the style and durability of books, a useful but rather impersonal cause. Now I was in a movement aimed at helping people.

Active in the Guild from the beginning was a variety of men and women from many backgrounds, working at all levels in the industry. We even had a few from old-money New York families. Their education ranged from high school dropouts to a degree in the esoteric study of Middle English held by a young woman who later became a union organizer. Some had radical parents; some, like me, had reacted against a conservative upbringing. These people had found, many for the first time, a place where they felt at home. There were no blacks (called Negroes in those days) because none were employed in our polite industry.

The Guild program included public discussions of questions, part literary and part political, that might attract and stimulate people in publishing. Sympathetic authors, some with big reputations, took part, both because we offered a forum for their ideas and because they wanted to help our organization. Sometimes they surprised us. One best-selling novelist, known as a tough and sophisticated fellow and creator of hard-boiled heroes, turned out to be in terror of appearing in public. When we led him to the speaker's platform he was in such a funk that he could not climb onto it.

One performer who had no such trepidations was Morris Ernst, a lawyer widely known for defending publishers against censorship. He told us how he had broken down, word by word, court rulings against the printing of four-letter words in such books as *Ulysses* and *Lady Chatterly's Lover*. "There's an old agricultural term," he said, "used in English literature since the Middle Ages." At our meeting was a group of retired schoolteachers who did editorial work on children's books and who were enthusiastic new Guild members. It was obvious that Ernst would eventually utter that ancient word, but the four women waited until he finally said, "and the word is fuck." They then gathered up their wraps and left. We thought we had lost them forever, but they came again another day and stayed with the Guild for a long time.

The Guild set up a school with classes in publishing skills such as manuscript copyediting and ad writing. I transferred my own course in book design from Columbia University and taught it at the Guild for ten or twelve years.

On the social side we had parties, both to get to know one another and to attract supporters. Some of the people I met at these parties became lifelong friends. One of these was James Marston Fitch, a magazine editor from Tennessee who later became an eminent architectural historian, Columbia professor, and author of *American Building*, a brilliant history. Another was James Hansen, married to a British literary agent. He was an engineer from South Dakota, concerned all his life with aspects of building construction, and resident for some years in a house he built on my farm.

A third was a struggling playwright from Brooklyn named Arthur Miller, whose first wife, Mary Slattery, worked for Harper's. Miller wrote parts of his early plays at the farm, and I saw him often after he came to live near me in Roxbury. Later I became a friend and confidant of his second wife, Marilyn Monroe, about whose beauty, vulnerability, and sensitive intelligence too much has been written—some of it by people who never knew her. Arthur has a passion for growing trees, which of course touches me. Our relations have had some warm and cool periods, but after nearly sixty years we are still friends.

People in the Guild, sharing strong feelings and working toward serious objectives, naturally developed intense emotional relations. They were mostly young people, and in the free atmosphere many sexual liaisons resulted. These did not always survive the fierce arguments on Guild policy and strategy. It was not always clear whether a disagreement came from personal or ideological differences. On the whole, however, everyone was remarkably amicable and cooperative.

The Guild existed for two years in this pre-union stage, making no effort to carry on collective bargaining with publishers, our membership limited to employees whose work was defined as "peculiar to the publishing industry." There was at the time an Office Workers Union for clerks, receptionists, stenographers, and bookkeepers, some of them in publishing jobs. It was understood that if we were to become an industrial union we would join with them, and the union would then represent everyone from porter to secretary to editor.

The concept of industrial unionism had grown as American industry grew. Huge new companies like General Motors were employing workers with a variety of skills who were members of many separate craft unions. In a large automobile plant, for example, there were machinists, electricians, sheet-metal workers, carriage builders, rubber workers, and dozens of others, each of these trades represented by a craft union that had its origin in the nineteenth century. This fragmentation made it impossible for employees to bargain on an equal basis with corporation managers.

Soon after the First World War a group of the more progressive union leaders in the American Federation of Labor (AFL), led by United Mine Workers president John L. Lewis, set up the Committee for Industrial Organization to help unionize the new industries. Lewis was a powerful personality who had led the miners to many victories in the labor wars of the twenties and thirties. Today he is remembered as one of the giants in American labor history. Many officials of the old AFL craft unions, fearing the loss of members and power, opposed these leaders' efforts to form industrial unions and expelled them from the federation. In 1935 the Committee became the Congress of Industrial Organizations (CIO), and the AFL and CIO operated as a dual federation for many years.

In 1935, during the first Roosevelt administration, Congress passed the National Labor Relations Act, aimed at furthering labor's participation in the economic recovery and protecting unions against antilabor violence. The landmark General Motors sit-in strike in early 1936 was followed by the first United Auto Workers contract in July 1937.

The CIO, once firmly established, extended its organizing drive to cover so-called white-collar employees and encouraged the formation of the United Office and Professional Workers (UOPWA), joining unions of people employed in financial, insurance, advertising, publishing, and other business establishments, social service agencies, and even a militant group of commercial and fine artists, with the famous illustrator Rockwell Kent as their energetic president. The Book and Magazine Guild became Local 18 of the UOPWA but retained its old name.

At this time I was president of the Guild, and I held that position for more than six years. I found I had some aptitude for organizing, strategy, and publicity, and my reputation in the publishing field was an asset. Also, now that I had something real to talk about I lost my self-consciousness on the platform and could speak easily in meetings. I had never before had the experience of meeting with groups to discuss problems and make decisions. I learned what many know, that such meetings stimulate thinking, broaden understanding, produce new ideas; they do not simply serve, as I had naively thought, to collect opinions and form majorities.

Once the Guild became a full-fledged union we set about organizing in earnest. We persuaded groups of publishing workers to meet at our headquarters, we distributed union leaflets at the doors of their offices, we held "demonstrations" to make our presence known. Publishers were rather paternal and their employees fairly content with their jobs and slow to perceive that their interests might be opposed to the interests of their bosses. Our first successes were in offices where management was known to have liberal ideas and a tendency to hire politically progressive people, and we also drew members from nonprofit publishing enterprises.

We won a number of elections under the regulations of the National Labor Relations Act which entitled us to negotiate contracts with management. Part of my responsibility was to participate in negotiating these contracts. I found that the more liberal the owners were, the more they clung to their paternalistic practices. Dealing with them about salaries was not so difficult, but on questions such as grievance procedures, sick leave, and equalizing Christmas bonuses, they hated to relinquish the right to deal with each employee on a personal basis and to accept standard union rules for equal treatment of everybody. They wanted their good intentions appreciated, and they wanted to feel each employee's personal gratitude for the benefits they dispensed.

Some of the Guild members worked on publications of nonprofit organizations such as the Foreign Policy Association. Negotiating a union contract, I sometimes found myself facing board members who were pillars of the establishment, lawyers or bankers, people who knew my family. I must admit I enjoyed these confrontations. It was a time when such people liked to denounce Franklin Roosevelt as a traitor to his class, and here was I, a small bore traitor, appearing in an adversary position and questioning their benevolence.

Although the Guild did not succeed in organizing the larger, more conservative publishing offices, our presence in the industry brought benefits to thousands who had never joined us. It was generally agreed that we were entitled to credit for improvements in salaries, in the change to a five-day week where five-and-a-half had been standard, and in smoothing worker-management relations.

As could be expected, my conspicuous place in the Guild was not uniformly admired by my publisher clients. Those who were strongly opposed to their employees joining a union did not want my access to their offices to be taken as a sign of sympathy for the Guild, and this began to lower my income. Partly in recognition of this, and partly as an affirmation of the Guild's support of high professional standards in publishing, a dinner was held in March 1941, announced as a celebration of my twenty years in the industry. It was held at the old Woodstock Hotel in New York; tickets cost $1.25.

This turned out to be the most gratifying, indeed the most flattering thing that had ever happened to me. There was a large sponsoring committee including thirteen editor, writer, and artist friends of mine, three eminent printers, three CIO union presidents, and eight partners in publishing firms for whom I designed books. Well over two hundred people came to the party and signed the guest list, mostly people from publishing and printing but also my surviving grandmother and her sister from Bridgeport.

There were the customary speeches, and my response was a somewhat emotional and not highly successful effort to show the connection between good design and economic order in the industry. I had said before that "the designer's first job is to help bring order and repose into our physical world." I was trying to say that evening that I saw economic order as part of that pattern and that economic justice could not be omitted from it.

A souvenir book was distributed at the dinner with essays by Helen Kingery, secretary of the Guild, on my union labors; by Percy Seitlin, a frequent critic of printing, on my typographic ideas and style; and by Philip Van Doren Stern, a book designer turned author, on how my background and personality bore on my activities in design and in the union. Stern wrote, in part: "Long training in printing craft technique which calls for orderliness of working method, has imbued in him a great respect for efficiency and economy of means. He believes in creating the best possible product with the least amount of human wear and tear. He is convinced that the machine must be the servant and not the master of man. Interested as he is in mechanical methods, he is more interested in human values. It can be said of him what Thoreau said of John Brown: 'He would have left a Greek accent slanting the wrong way and righted up a falling man.'" As I write these memoirs over fifty years later, I am still touched by those words.

It took me a long time to get my feet back on the ground after that event! I was president of the Guild for another year or two, but the leadership was gradually being taken over by full-time organizers. After Pearl Harbor the war became everyone's paramount concern, and by 1944 I had no more union responsibilities. I had no part in structural changes in the CIO after the war, and these are not part of my story. I do know that the Guild eventually became a local of another white-collar union, larger than the UOPWA and with a more conservative orientation. Unionism in publishing was dormant for some years. Later there was a drive by Harper employees to organize, and the Guild was cited as precedent. Although I went to speak at one tumultuous Harper meeting, I could take no further part, and I cannot say now how the effort ended.

My years in the Guild changed me in ways that I could not perceive at the time. I had always been a determined individualist, no doubt quite self-absorbed. As the Guild developed into a full-fledged trade union and became a unit in the huge CIO, it was exciting to be part of a movement that was changing the world. I had to give up some of my cherished independence to participate in union activities, but it was worth it. I was giving up some of my freedom for independent action (which had only limited value) but not my freedom for independent thought. And if I was losing a little of my belief in my own uniqueness, that was well lost. I was certainly aware that I was increasing my capacity to contribute to group movements, a capacity that was to be useful to me for the rest of my life.

One inevitable result of my deep involvement in the Book and Magazine Guild was an attachment which developed during the last unhappy days of my marriage to Jane. I was working every day with a Guild member named Helen Thompson, a handsome, self-possessed, and very competent Californian, once married and divorced, living with her mother in New York. When the work of the Guild expanded she became its first full-time executive secretary, and as our friendship evolved I became her full-time companion. The Guild had become a central part of my life; she was sharing that and also many other interests. After my divorce we talked now and then about marriage.

The end, when it came, was like an episode in a soap opera. Helen was deeply devoted to the union, and being a highly emotional person, she was feeling intense pressure from her job. As her mentor and superior in the organization I came to personify those pressures, though I tried to share them.

She got acquainted, through routine union dealings, with Bennet Cerf, a partner in Random House, with which the Guild had a union contract. She agreed, rashly, to go with him to a number of dinner and weekend parties as a relief from the stresses and responsibilities of her job. Her new friend was a superficial fellow, successful in his business but overeager for publicity and a tireless celebrity hunter. Possibly he was intrigued by the novelty of knowing a real live union organizer and exhibiting her to his friends. He was surely a most unlikely person to lure Helen from her dedication to the welfare of publishing workers, but that is what happened. She resigned from her Guild job; when she announced her defection it caused a bit of a scandal and a lot of embarrassment for me.

After a few months Helen went back to California and presently married an old suitor there. I was not easily consoled; I had again got myself deeply involved with an emotionally unstable person, in spite of what I thought I had learned earlier. It was some years before I recovered completely from the collapse of my hopes for a new life with what had seemed to be an ideal partner.

Surfacing from my deep immersion, I began to look up old friends, among them Eileen and Ruth McKenney. Eileen was a lost lady, in the style of many nineteenth-century heroines. She had the misfortune of being the ravishingly beautiful younger sister of a talented, overweight, plain-faced but vivacious achiever who dominated her from infancy. Ruth was the author of humorous stories about the adventures of two young Ohio women working in New York. Eileen's charms were the cause of most of their adventures, but somehow her beauty was always made to seem a handicap and to emphasize her perplexity in coping with reality.

I thought her touching and found comfort for a short time in her company and in her bed. Recently divorced, she had been persuaded by Ruth to let her infant son go to live with his father in California, but she soon went west herself to be near the child, and I never saw her again. She fell in love with a brilliant, reckless young writer named Nathanael West, notorious for hard drinking and fast driving. They were married and within a year were both killed in a highway smashup. Ruth's *My Sister Eileen* stories became a long-running Broadway play and then a popular movie.

I had long since learned that females were no less interested than males in acknowledging their sexual feelings and in indulging them freely if they felt like doing so. This was especially true, as one might expect, of young women I met in the labor movement who were questioning the economic and social beliefs of their families. For a time I had more sexual encounters than I want to list. I found, however, that for some years after the jolt of Helen Thompson's exit I could respond physically but not emotionally to a companion. Needless to say, this did not make me a very satisfactory romantic partner.

I became a close friend of an editor and novelist I met in the Guild, a delightful and stimulating young woman. Her feelings for me developed an intensity which I was unable to match. In her next novel I appeared as an industrial designer and dairy farmer, clearly identified by quotations from things I had written. I was depicted as rather dashing but thoroughly self-centered and undependable, which from her viewpoint I undoubtedly was. I guess I was eventually forgiven, for later in life we became very good friends.

From an experience or two during my marriage, I learned that infidelity gave me no feelings of guilt, that my relations with a third person could be, in my mind, entirely detached from any other commitment. I know that this is against the rules. I have seen that people who break the rules usually pay in the end; indeed, I myself have certainly not escaped. I think I am moral and responsible in most of my dealings with others, but monogamy and fidelity are not clearly written in my rule book. I do not assume that simply stating this can nullify the judgments of people I have hurt.

I wish I could avoid discussing this side of my character—only a novelist of talent could handle the subject without sounding mawkish. I hope I am not by this confession seeming to claim some kind of reverse nobility.

Winston Churchill once said, "Any man who is not a Socialist before he is forty has no heart; and a man who is a Socialist after forty has no head." Only someone who lived through the turmoil of the thirties can fully understand why so many people were convinced that a basic change in the economic system was the only hope for the survival of democracy. Seeing how vulnerable to economic change my family's apparent financial stability really was, and how fragile the economy of the book business, fed my disillusion with capitalism. The 1927 execution in Massachusetts of Sacco and Vanzetti, poor immigrant anarchists widely believed to be falsely accused of murder because of their radical beliefs, was a milestone in national political enlightenment.

The Democratic administration of Franklin D. Roosevelt was not elected until 1932, after more than three years of President Hoover's ineffectual efforts to help the economy, years during which he in fact denied that any crisis existed. By that time, the extent of bank failures, business bankruptcies, unemployment, and spreading poverty and despair had made it certain that the new administration's elaborate plans to revive the country would take many years to succeed, if they ever could.

In 1931 and 1932, with unemployment and hunger increasing, there were police assaults on crowds of people demanding food. In Washington, D.C., the U.S. Army attacked a huge march by veterans demanding payment of cash bonuses promised for their service in the First World War, killing some of them. Police and company-hired thugs were using violence to prevent union organization in many cities, and in 1934 there was a general strike in San Francisco.

In Europe Fascist dictators, first Benito Mussolini in Italy after 1922 then Adolf Hitler in Germany after 1933, were destroying democratic institutions, opposition political parties, cooperatives, and trade unions and were moving against racial minorities and modern movements in the arts. Fascism was offering one kind of cure for all the world's ills, but millions of people of goodwill were looking toward socialism as a more humane alternative. The 1917 revolution in Russia had produced what seemed to be a stable new society, a form of socialism called communism, with ideals of equality and social justice. This seemed to me and to many others of my generation to offer hope.

There had been a socialist movement in the United States since the middle of the nineteenth century. The labor movement had always included socialists, anarchists, and other species and degrees of radicals. Many of these people joined the Communist party when it spread west from the Soviet Union after 1917. So also did writers, artists, philosophers, and other creative workers who had traditionally shunned politics. Some of these were my friends.

I was of course aware from the beginning that left-wing people in the union movement had taken the lead in promoting the idea of industrial unionism and in the effort to organize employees in the industry where I was working. These same people were also in the forefront of the struggle against fascism. I was impressed with their zeal and dedication, and I learned that some of them were members of the Communist party. They were working for goals I believed in; I could see no reason not to join them, and after a while I did. I was a member of the party for several years; my only commitment was to work for the growth and effectiveness of the Book and Magazine Guild.

Political debate was an important part of union life in those days; to join a union was a political as well as an economic decision. Many union people, both officials and rank and file, were strong supporters of the Soviet Union, though all believers in socialism did not admire Stalin. Leon Trotsky, one of the leaders of the revolution, broke with Stalin and was exiled in 1929. To Trotsky's followers Stalin was a betrayer of the revolution. There was a small group of dedicated Trotskyists in the Guild led by Mary McCarthy, a pretty young editor I knew in the Covici-Friede office. Support for the Soviet Union by Guild members was fiercely denounced by them in ways that sometimes disrupted our meetings. It was my duty as chairman to keep the peace, and apparently that earned me McCarthy's lasting enmity. In her novel *The Group*, published nearly twenty years later, there is a very minor character referred to as "Jacoby, another Stalinist, a book designer."

I have always regretted this episode. As time passed and I had second thoughts about the Stalin regime, and when McCarthy's admiration for Trotsky may have faded, I wished we had become friends. I not only enjoyed her writing but found that I agreed with many of her prejudices, particularly with her frank contempt for certain writers we both knew.

Toward the end of my six years as Guild president I lost some of my enthusiasm for working with the more fervid of my fellow members. As strongly as I felt about the union and its objectives, I could not match their single-minded devotion to the class struggle. I had a few unhappy experiences with what in the labor movement was called "super-leftism."

On one typical occasion there was a meeting of a large group from Dutton, one of the old-line conservative publishers. These people had been persuaded to meet with us for a preliminary discussion of the idea of joining the Guild. By that time the Guild had grown to have two professional organizers, and they, in a burst of what I thought was excessive radical zeal, were urging these uncommitted people to picket the Dutton office in support of an organizing strategy. This seemed to me unwise and unworkable, and as president of the Guild I was able to assert my authority to veto the plan. The two organizers were of course unhappy about my action. They took it as evidence that I was not truly devoted to working-class interests, and they made an effort to reduce my standing and influence in the Guild.

Incidents like this were causing me to lose confidence in the judgment of some of the leftist unionists I was working with and in the likelihood of our eventual success in organizing the bulk of publishing workers. Perhaps my attachment to the labor movement was more intellectual than emotional, but I suspect that my approach would have taken us further toward our goal. Meanwhile my work as a designer, my only source of income, continued to take time and energy. The farm needed more attention each year, and my responsibilities for my daughter Maria also grew. All this was making union activity more difficult.

As to my social thinking, I lost confidence in the political judgment of my fellow left-wing union activists long before I lost confidence in the future of the Soviet undertaking. I had managed to swallow the bitter potion offered to party members by the 1939 Stalin-Hitler nonaggression pact, though it cost me some friends. Later the stupendous achievement of the Soviet armies in defeating the Nazis in Russia restored my admiration for Soviet power, if not for Soviet doctrine.

I had seen, however, that in a few short years the romantic optimism, the hope for a society free of all restraints except those rooted in the natural goodness of humanity, was losing its innocence. As had occurred in other revolutionary movements, the idealism of many of the most devoted people I knew was gradually being debased, first by factionalism, then by intolerance and fanaticism. What one observer called "the wreckage that unrestrained moral intensity can create" was their final reward.

I was beginning to doubt the possibility that socialism could solve America's problems. The reforms of Roosevelt's New Deal, beginning to show signs of accomplishing what had earlier seemed impossible, made it look as if our system had more strength and resilience than I thought and that it could be more humane. I began to see that Marx's theories were being at least partly invalidated by developments in American society. The growth of trade union power between the two wars had somewhat blunted the edge of economic exploitation, the extraction of surplus value created by workers, which Marx thought would destroy capitalism. What Marx meant, of course, was that if a five-dollar-a-day worker produced ten dollars worth of goods, the surplus five dollars going to the boss would eventually cause an imbalance in the economy which the system could not support.

From my experience in a major cultural enterprise I began to see that to a large extent economic exploitation was being replaced by a process of cultural exploitation. The spread of advertising and propaganda, in print and in the new electronic media, coupled with the invention and production of new consumer goods and packaged entertainment, was convincing people that more and more possessions and luxuries were the keys to a good life. The sale of goods to gullible consumers was bringing more wealth to the owning class than the simple extraction of surplus value from the person who produced the goods could possibly yield.

Early in the century this new trend became apparent. The later efforts of Roosevelt's New Deal to stimulate the economy by raising both the earning power of workers and the profitability of business speeded up its development. What was not yet a factor in the thirties, of course, was the enormous ability of television to bring the market into the home. Gradually the ingenious talents of the advertising agencies, using music, visual stunts, subliminal effects, and snippets of drama, have made the selection and purchase of merchandise a central American preoccupation. This has gone so far that in the 1980s the General Motors Corporation, which some years before had admitted slipping low-priced Chevrolet engines into their higher-priced cars, was advertising its new Chevrolets as "the heartbeat of America." How much farther can cynicism go?

Although I lost most of my faith in socialism and Marxist theory as the answer to my questions, I did not lose my skepticism about the ability of laissez-faire capitalism, however disguised as "free enterprise," to provide everyone with a decent life. Even when not carried to extremes of greed and heartlessness, as under the Reagan and Bush presidencies, inadequate social planning and the power of property have left us with needless poverty and inequality and a shamefully degraded environment.

As I have always known, however, I very much need to be part of a social structure in which I can find an outlet for my energies, in which, as I had said years before, I can have a realistic hope of shaping for myself the sort of world I want to live in. This urge to act is for me a very powerful one; where there is a choice between ideas and action, between advocating and participating, I will choose the latter.

For some years I had found in the Guild and the labor movement scope for my energies and a rewarding sense of being part of a worthwhile enterprise. The situation was changing, however; a guild of amateurs was becoming inevitably a union led by professional organizers. They were no less devoted to the interests of our members, but it was increasingly clear that the days of my working with them and making an effective contribution to the labor movement were coming to an end.

I have no regrets about my earlier decision to join with the communists in working toward goals I believed in. I have always remembered the gratification that came from working with dedicated people for an ideal. I have seen some of the people who once shared that ideal turn their backs on it, beat their breasts in public repentance, in effect spit on their own pasts. I am proud to say that I have never done that.

My left-wing experience was common to so many of my generation that questions about it have for many years seemed out-of-date and irrelevant. As far as I can recall, I was never asked in public whether I had ever been a communist until 1986 when I was a Democratic candidate for the Connecticut legislature. I had run for that same office in 1944 on the ticket headed by Franklin Roosevelt.

At a 1986 political meeting a Republican woman, known as a factional battler within her own party, asked me whether I had ever been a communist. I recalled that in the days of Joe McCarthy and J. Edgar Hoover agents of the FBI had come to see me on one of their fishing expeditions and had planted a few rumors about me in Bethel. After over forty years as a registered Democrat, I had no intention of being diverted from a discussion of real issues by a question from someone who had not the slightest understanding of what life was like in the 1930s, and who was resurrecting an ancient device for discrediting a political opponent. I was unwilling to use my limited platform time for a long explanation of my motives and actions in the distant past, and I said "No" to the woman, which was all the reply her hostility and ignorance deserved. I have never regretted this prevarication.

Although this direct confrontation was for me unique, the assumption that radical ideas and left-wing associations are somehow shameful is not unique. "Any stigma will do to beat a dogma" is a famous double pun. The stigma of implied communist sympathies is still used against ideas, where logic will not work. In 1988 the Philip Morris tobacco company was suggesting in its publicity that people opposed to cigarette advertising *might* be communist sympathizers, and George Bush in his campaign for the presidency in 1988 was not above using a similar insinuation to discredit his opponent.

9 🍎 A Time of Transition

At the onset of World War II in 1941 major changes were taking place in my life. The collapse of my family, beginning in 1926, was assured by the death of my mother in 1940. My marriage to Jane was over, my prospects for another marriage unrealized. It was already clear that my strenuous days in the labor movement would end in a few years. My continuing responsibilities would be for Maria, for the farm, and of course for my career as a book designer.

The breakup of my immediate family began as early as 1926. My father, Edward, who had always been in good physical health in spite of his behavior problems, suddenly collapsed. After thirty years the effects of his syphilis infection had finally caught up with him. He suffered what was called a nervous breakdown, a term applied in those days to a variety of poorly understood neurological disorders. The shock of this new development was added to the distress my mother, Clarice, had for so long endured.

My father was forced to give up his produce business and sell his share to his partner, George Cook. The brownstone house on 77th Street was sold, my parents moved with my sister to a small apartment, and I went to my own place on 51st Street. My brother was away in New Jersey at a military school. My father dabbled a bit in real estate, a field which had always interested him, but had almost no income, and my grandfather Spero had to support my parents. Needless to say, this was humiliating and intensified Ed's neurotic behavior.

They bought a place in Mt. Kisco in Westchester with a modest house, a small cottage for my then-invalid grandfather and his nurse, and another cottage for my sister, Marian, and her husband to use as a summer retreat. We all expected that Clarice would outlive Ed and enjoy the tranquillity she had never had with him. Marian and I once suggested discreetly that she leave him, but it was clear that her feelings of duty and pity outweighed her need for self-preservation, and we gave up that effort.

Added to her other troubles, my mother was distressed about the breakup of my marriage to Jane, whom she liked, and worried about the welfare of her granddaughter Maria. She could not completely accept my way of life. I remember one day when she called me at the farm to come to see her because she was miserable and needed comfort. Yet when I quit my work and rushed to Mt. Kisco she greeted me by saying, in the midst of all her distress, "Why do you come here dressed like a workman?" I thought it extraordinary how her early notions of propriety could persist through all her trials. It was another sign of the tenacious adherence to the rules of her upbringing which made her stay by the man she had chosen so many years before.

In 1931 my sister married a Wall Street statistician named Lewis Fisher, an economist rather than a trader. Marian was tall, solid, and humorous, athletic when few girls cared to be, and rather like me in temperament. When she married Lewis she was working in a fancy department store, and they lived the life of typical suburban commuters. After some years they quit their city jobs and converted a large old house on a back road in Morris, Connecticut, into a small inn, with some dealing in antique furniture as a sideline. Marian was a superb cook and manager and an amiable hostess; without advertising they kept the inn filled with compatible people. Their son, John, went to Harvard on a scholarship. Later he became a partner in a small educational publishing firm producing audiovisual guidance and instructional materials. Lewis died suddenly in 1964, and Marian returned to live in Westchester and expand her antique business. Now in her late eighties, she can barely see but is courageous and amazingly good-humored.

My brother, Willard, known as Billy, was not so solid; he was handsome and charming but self-indulgent. After a spotty academic career he eloped with a girl of sixteen who wanted to be a movie star. They settled in Hollywood where he became an actor's agent, and he managed to acquire three more wives before he died of a heart attack in 1967, leaving two sons from his third marriage. He had no tolerance at all for his father, perhaps because they shared some of the same weaknesses, and once shocked us all by striking him at a family gathering. I saw little of him during his Hollywood years; even on his business trips to the East he seldom managed to find time to visit his family.

Clarice had no sisters. Her one brother, Arthur, always called Archie, was an amiable extrovert like his father but not nearly as competent. After he had tried other fields, he was staked by his father to a stock exchange seat. That was before the boom of the early twenties, and seats were still moderate in cost. Archie had a talent for making friends, and that was all he needed to make money in those days. Grandpa was getting old and losing touch with the world; he only knew that his son seemed to have the key to Wall Street. Like many others in those boom times, Archie went deep into debt for funds to play the market.

When the 1929 crash came he was wiped out, and with his money went much of his father's. With his limited understanding of economic reality and his hopeful faith in Herbert Hoover's famous cry that prosperity was "just around the corner," Archie's advice continued to reduce his father's worth. Grandpa's prosperity did not survive him. At his death in 1938 his estate proved to be much smaller than expected.

As for my own finances, I had little urge, and perhaps little talent, for making money, and I was living a Spartan life. I cannot say that I relished that, yet I had chosen to do what I was doing and certainly did not think of myself as a victim of misfortune. I was reminded of the old saying, "shirtsleeves to shirtsleeves in three generations." My grandfather had risen from a poor childhood to a wealthy middle age, his children enjoyed ease and security, and I, his grandson, was living in a shabby farmhouse and holding on to the bottom rung of the economic ladder.

In 1940, a year before the bombing of Pearl Harbor took the United States into the Second World War, my mother died in Mexico City. She was stricken with a rare tropical fever and was ill for only a short time. She and my father had been traveling frequently. She seemed to find him more relaxed and agreeable when he was

Clarice, 1940

away from any competition for her attention and from the very evident affection everyone had for her. She was only fifty-eight when she died, healthy and vigorous, and Edward had not completely recovered from his "nervous breakdown."

Her firstborn, I had been close to my mother as a child and young man, but somehow her death when I was thirty-seven was not very real to me. It happened when she was far away in another country; I did not see her die. She had left on a routine vacation trip, but suddenly she was gone. She had become remote, absorbed in trying to make the best of her unhappy life with my father. There seemed to be no way I could help her, and I was not sure she really understood what kind of man I had become.

Unfortunately, she did not live to attend the Guild dinner in 1941. It was the sort of symbolic event which would have made more acceptable to her what she thought of as my erratic career. She also did not live to know my second wife, Martha, who is like her in many ways and would have been a great comfort to her. My father lived for twenty-one years after my mother's death. His neurotic condition led to increasingly aberrant behavior, which I do not care to describe. He finally died in a nursing home in Torrington, Connecticut, in 1961.

My mother was the last of the Speros as far as I was concerned. My grandfather had left his family behind when he came to New York as a boy. By the time I knew him he was in his fifties, and he never talked about his childhood in Syracuse. Two young Spero cousins came to visit when I was a child, but they disappeared. My uncle Arthur and his wife both died at middle age, leaving two adopted children whom I never really knew. Grandma Spero had one brother, Uncle Harry, a small, elegant bachelor with a high, cracked voice who had never left the nineteenth century. He had no skills for coping with life's realities, and Grandpa was rather scornful of him.

The Josephys, in contrast to the Speros, were very much a thriving clan. My grandmother Gertrude was in constant touch with her Bridgeport relatives, her four children and all their families, and countless other kinfolk scattered about the country and in Europe. Most of the Josephys had long lives, so their ranks were always full. Grandma made sure to have plenty of them at her frequent parties. She lived to be eighty-six, which was old for her generation. Her two daughters died in their late nineties, and even my father, with all his illnesses, lived to be eighty-four.

There was a huge gathering of Josephy relatives on my aunt Hortense Brodek's ninetieth birthday, but that was the last attempt to continue Gertrude's program for maintaining family solidarity. I certainly have not made much effort; of my many cousins, the only one I see frequently is Alvin Josephy, Jr., a writer, an authority on the American Indian, and an ardent environmentalist. We are friends because we have a lot to talk about and not because we are related.

When the Japanese attacked Pearl Harbor in Hawaii on December 7, 1941, I was still president of the Guild and of course still a dedicated anti-Fascist. America was finally forced to end its pretense of neutrality, and I was relieved that we were joining the war. The majority of Americans had been convinced since the Nazis first invaded Poland that we would eventually have to take part.

There was, however, a powerful organization called America First which appealed to those who wanted us to sit out the war. Some of them thought it had been a mistake to get into the First World War and believed we should stay out of this one. Others, many of them influential, were open or secret admirers of Fascist ideas. They hated Roosevelt's support of labor, social security, and other liberal policies and thought that a bit of fascism was just what we needed.

The decision was made for us by the bombing of Pearl Harbor. I first learned of the attack from the shouts of men selling "extras" on a New York street. These were special editions of newspapers, the usual way of spreading sensational news before people came to depend on the radio.

We were obliged to fight both in the Pacific and in Europe. This required a far greater engagement of our human and economic resources than did the First World War a quarter century earlier. I was already eleven years old when World War I began, old enough to see that it had only a limited effect on our daily lives. World War II was different; there was strict rationing of many commodities, tight control of industrial production, and pressure on farmers to grow more food.

When we entered the war I was thirty-eight, a few months too old to be drafted for the army or the navy. After considerable soul-searching I decided not to volunteer. The farm was producing food, but, in its early stage of development, producing very little money, and there was no one but me to take care of it. Maria needed both attention and support. I had to keep my two-room flat in the city while she was at school there and be available to her even when she was supposed to be staying with her mother. If I had given up my income from publishers, there was no way I could have managed.

American trade unions were united in supporting the war effort. In 1942 I was appointed to serve on a citizens' draft board in New York. The unions were concerned because most draft boards were staffed by comfortable businessman types, and it was reported that many of their decisions seemed to be influenced by class bias. Mayor La Guardia was asked to appoint more union people; he asked for names, and mine was on the union list. I was legally a resident of Connecticut, but that didn't seem to matter. I did indeed find that well-washed, well-spoken young men were being given more lenient treatment by the board.

I remember one incident when four brothers, all of draft age, appeared before us. Two were unemployed, the others had low-paying jobs. They had come to ask that two of them be deferred from service because their widowed mother was dependent on them. We agreed to consider their appeal. When they were leaving we heard the loud explosions of a car motor. These boys had managed, in spite of their poverty, to gain a little freedom and mobility by buying an old automobile. My fellow board members were enraged by their shamelessness, and we voted four to one to send them all to the army. I stayed on the board until I went to work at the Stratford forge and was able to modify a little the prejudices of my colleagues.

Betty Bacon, a union friend of mine, asked me one day, "What are you doing to help fight fascism?" I agreed I was not doing all I could. After so many years of antifascist political agitation I now had a chance to do more than talk, and I decided to look for a part-time war production job. I found a government employment bureau eager to make use of my six-foot, two-hundred-pound body. Bethel and Danbury were chiefly hat manufacturing towns; felt hats were not needed for fighting the war, and the hat shops were shut down because they could not be converted to producing anything essential. I was sent to the Patterson forge in Stratford, near

Bridgeport, twenty-five or thirty miles from the farm. They needed muscle and assigned me to a crew of four unskilled men working with an experienced forger. My pay was ninety cents an hour.

My boss was a Belgian who could do amazing things to white-hot steel billets with a huge steam-powered hammer and a few simple shaping tools. I learned how to maneuver heavy bars of steel into and out of furnaces with the help of a chain hoist and how to pick up and throw smaller pieces with a four-foot pair of tongs. We heated our lunches on the hot steel which lay all around on the floor. My shop nickname was Farmer; when the men learned I grew fruit, some of them ordered apples, delivered to them at the forge.

After a while Patterson's needed someone to work at night tending milling machines. My new job was to set the automatic machines, and while they were cutting away at pieces of steel I had time to read or to work on book-design problems. The foreman once asked me what I was doing, and I said it was homework for a correspondence school course I was taking.

Patterson's was a second-rate shop, but any plant could get contracts for war work. The parts we forged and machined seemed properly made; we could only guess for what they would be used. There were no safety rules or devices and no comforts for us, no place to rest away from the intense heat, too few showers, too few lockers. There was only the satisfaction of doing something for the war effort.

I suspected that some of the men there had been deferred from serving in the armed forces because they were doing vital work at the forge. That may be why they felt obliged to act tough. There was a bordello across the street staffed by black women, and some of the men liked to insist on the old macho-racist notion that going there would change your luck. Few of them, however, were as tough as they pretended to be.

It was the most demanding period of my life, with little time for reading and little repose for thinking. I would go down to the forge in my old pickup truck. After work I would park it at the Bridgeport railroad station and go to New York. Next day I would see a few clients with my typographic layouts, attend a Guild meeting or have a date with a girlfriend, go back to the forge for another night shift, and then home to the farm to squeeze in a few hours' work there.

Toward the end of the war I left to do a very different kind of war work. My friend Ben Shahn was in charge of the graphics in a CIO support-the-war propaganda program. Ben was a well-known painter and graphic artist with strong leftist principles. He believed that the place for the artist was in the social struggle, not in the sheltered atmosphere of the studio and the art gallery. He asked me to help him with the design of leaflets and advertising matter, and I left Patterson's to do that. This commitment took all the time I could spare and finally ended my years in the Guild and in radical politics.

During the war years there was plenty to do at the farm. The orchard I planted in 1935 was coming into bearing; first the peaches which have some fruit at three years, then the apples a few years later. Before the war I had cleared rocks and prepared the soil for two more orchards, each somewhat smaller than the first, and planted apples there. They would not bear fruit until after the war, but the trees had to be pruned and sprayed to keep them growing properly.

It was not until the end of the war that Americans fully learned the whole truth about the Nazis' annihilation of most of the Jews in Europe. Why people here, Jews and Gentiles alike, were insulated from knowledge of the Holocaust is an incredible part of the history of the war, but it is not part of my personal story. Of course I was aware, as was everyone, of some of what was happening. I had even heard that some of my distant German relatives had "disappeared," but somehow it all seemed only an incidental part of the whole horror.

By the end of the war I was ready to become a full-time citizen of Bethel. I had to travel to New York regularly, and occasionally to other cities, to see publishers about books I was designing, but I made these trips as a commuter. I had no more ties to the labor movement in New York, and Maria was at school at Carmel, twenty miles west of the farm.

The trees needed a lot more of my time. My first orchard was producing substantial quantities of apples and peaches which had to be harvested and marketed. I planted two additional orchards, and my original acreage was more than doubled. And having been single since 1937, and having more time to think than I had during the war, what I was thinking about seriously was marriage. Twice during the war I was on the verge of making a proposal.

December 7, 1941, a date which Franklin Roosevelt said will live in infamy, also has for me one pleasant memory. I spent the evening in the company of a witty young children's book editor with a spectacular figure. She soon plunged into an affair with me as if she was seeking a new experience and thought I could provide it. We were close friends for about a year. Her father was a famous microbiologist, and before our amiable relations became too serious, I realized that she had hopes for a life in high academic circles and that I could never fulfill them or satisfy the ambitions of her domineering mother. We parted friends, and she eventually married a British physicist who won a Nobel prize. Then, to the delight of her mother, her father won a Nobel too.

Toward the end of the war I spent two years in pursuit of a dazzling young Pennsylvania woman with a delightful speaking voice who worked for one of my clients. We became close and affectionate friends, sharing many ideas and attitudes, and I began to think that our felicity might be permanent. The thought of marrying me frightened her, however, both because of our eighteen-year age difference and the prospect of her taking on a formidable twelve-year-old stepdaughter. Our relationship was broken off and then renewed several times. It was during one of those interludes that I became acquainted with Martha and finally ended my nine years of single life.

10 🍎 *A Long Marriage*

I first saw and admired Martha at a seashore place on
Fire Island when Maria and I were visiting Hardwick and Betty
Moseley there; then we met again on a train in Connecticut a year
or two later. Early in 1946 the Moseleys, who thought I had been
single too long (as did I by that time), told me that Martha had
finally ended a rough ten-year marriage and recommended her as
a perfect, and now available, mate for me. They arranged for the
two of us to go with them to some kind of publisher's party to get
further acquainted. That proved to be a brilliant bit of social engineering, a triumph of matchmaking, and the beginning of a six-
month courtship.

Martha Ann Davenport was born in 1912 in the cotton-mill and
peach-orchard town of Greer, in the northwest hills of South Carolina, called the Piedmont. The Davenports had the largest house
in Greer and a share of the chief business enterprises of the town.
As I learned later, the countryside was swarming with their relatives. Martha's father died when she was four and her mother ten
years later, an abandonment for which Martha never quite forgave
them. Two of her brothers had short lives also; the third, charming
but not very responsible, lived into his eighties.

She became the ward of her nine-years-older sister, Constance,
who had fallen in love with an Atlanta banker's son named Oscar
Earle Dooly. Earle took her as his bride to Miami, where the first

of several Florida booms was starting. Earle jumped aboard and presently became a leading figure in the business aristocracy. He was an enthusiastic trustee of the University of Miami, though it seemed to me when I knew him that he was more interested in football than in education.

Martha's early times as a prospective southern belle in the conventional churchgoing town of Greer ended at fourteen. She went to a private day school in Miami, then to Mt. Vernon Seminary, a finishing school in Washington, D.C., and to Rollins College in Florida. She was beginning to rebel against both the Greer and Miami cultures. A good liberal education at Rollins, with exposure to several outstanding teachers, completed her rebellion and fixed her sights on New York. When she reached twenty-one she was given an adequate allowance and went north to try for a career in the New York theater. She took speech lessons to get rid of her rich Piedmont accent and acting lessons in the Stanislavsky method from a Russian drama coach.

Aided by her exceptional good looks, she had some success getting parts in plays. She made friends among bright young writers and artists. One of them was William McCleery, who had come from Nebraska and was doing very well as a newspaper editor with Hearst, the Associated Press, and then the daily *PM*. He and Martha were married in 1936; it was a marriage that brought misfortunes from which Martha never completely recovered. She gave up her hopes for a career on the stage because she wanted to have children. Her first child, Thomas, was born severely mentally retarded and spent all of his short life in hospitals. Her second, Michael, was healthy and bright and has been a lifelong source of pleasure to her. Her third child, Jane, died suddenly in her crib at the age of two and a half.

McCleery was a slender reed for a young woman in trouble to lean on. When Jane died he left home for a while, leaving Martha and Michael to survive the shock without him. He wrote a play that ran some months on Broadway and then another. He quit newspaper work to be a full-time playwright, but he had little further success in the theater. After ten years of frustration Martha gave up. When I met her she had been seeing a psychoanalyst for three years.

She had lost her Southern accent but not her Southern charm or her concern for the people she had known in her childhood. She gave time and money to the movement for Negro civil rights long before that became a matter of wide national interest. She was on the board of the Southern Conference for Human Welfare, a combination of liberal political activists, union officials, and women who knew how to raise money for good causes.

Why did I want to marry Martha? Our backgrounds and histories were quite different, but somehow we had acquired experiences and a frame of reference which, together with respect for one another's intelligence and a shared need for family stability, made the prospect of a life together appealing. Added to this, she was an extremely pretty woman, and she had established instant rapport with Maria. Affectionate and generous, she possessed a talent for establishing sympathetic relations with all kinds of people. She was interested in all the arts, especially painting and sculpture. To me her taste seemed impeccable, which meant, of course, that we admired the same things. Her air of self-confidence seemed justified by her good looks and talent; it was only later that I became aware of the underlying fragility masked by her strong will.

Was I "in love" with Martha? After my fashion I certainly was. As before in my life, I was drawn to a volatile woman, capable of wide and sudden mood swings. I knew I was emotionally scarred by past unhappy experiences and in another way by nine years of mostly casual alliances. I wanted to end my period of single blessedness, but perhaps I was carrying more baggage than Martha should have been expected to handle.

I knew that she was first attracted to me because I was very different from Bill McCleery in my convictions, in my way of living, and even in my physique. She seemed impressed by my having enough energy for several unrelated Connecticut and New York activities. Ironically, the traits that attracted her were later among the very things that she resisted and finally rejected. Like many survivors of an unhappy marriage, she hesitated to try another one, but I finally persuaded her. I have told her many times that she is the best woman I ever knew. After forty-six years, many of them not too happy, I still think so.

In the spring of 1946 Martha went to Nevada to get her divorce, and on the last day of July we were married. She had an apartment on MacDougal Street in Greenwich Village, and the ceremony was performed there by a politically leftish young Methodist minister named Jack McMichael. Our oldest and best friends were all present, and it was a splendid party, marred only by the disappearance of Martha's silverware, apparently slipped out in the caterer's food containers.

We spent our honeymoon in a beach cottage on Fire Island, accompanied by Maria and Michael. That was not exactly the romantic thing to do, but it seemed appropriate for people of our age and sophistication. It also seemed a good way of strengthening quickly each child's ties to a new sibling.

We kept the MacDougal Street place for two years, then quit the city to live full-time at the farm. By then we had central heating there. We were anxious to have children—Martha had only Michael and I had Maria, then nearly thirteen and headed for the Putney School in Vermont where I had entered her the year before. Christina was born to us a year after our wedding and Ellen three years later.

Even before Ellen was born it was clear we needed to enlarge our house. I designed a substantial addition with some help from Henry Wright, an architect friend. The enlargement was a great success; it absorbed the old house into a New England–style structure but incorporated modern fenestration and heating and other practical innovations. We had a huge, cork-floored living room where children could ride bicycles and their parents could hold dances.

Martha was enthusiastic about her new life and excited at the prospect of some sisters or brothers for Mike. We went to visit her relatives in Greer, the first of many trips south. The big news among them was that Martha had married a Jew; the surprise seemed to be that I did not match any of their preconceptions. One elderly cousin, secure in her position and her prejudices, said she was glad to meet me and that she had expected I would be "small and dark."

At first Martha felt quite strange and isolated in Bethel. In 1949 she loaned her city friends Will and Sherley Roland money at 3 percent interest to buy the farm adjoining ours. My neighbor Everett Havens's wife had died, and he could not continue without her help. I planted a new orchard for Will and took care of the trees and crops in an older orchard that was on the farm. After six years the Rolands made what they considered an upward step socially and moved to Redding. Martha's financial help, and her dependence on them as neighbors, did not deter them. We bought their property, sold the house and buildings, and added the land to our farm.

When Martha and I were first married I was still deeply involved in the book business. When I became increasingly devoted to the farm, Martha had some doubts. She felt that working for publishers was a much superior vocation. In her early life she had acquired some illusions about the intellectual level of people in work related to the arts. I had always had friends who were writers and painters, but I was not impressed with the erudition or sophistication of the people I met in the book business. Martha, on the other hand, had no knowledge of agriculture and little respect for the people who were in it. This surprised me because in her South Carolina youth many of her friends and relatives were in some way involved with the management of farms. It was many years before she could see its possibilities as an intellectually demanding and rewarding pursuit and what it could mean to me. She herself loved gardening and knew a lot about plants, but she could not see that what was a hobby for her could become a major vocation for me.

Of course Martha and I had other differences. One that seemed minor to me but which has constantly troubled her is that I hate parlor games like backgammon and Scrabble, and she loves them. They give me such excruciating pain that I am almost physically unable to play. We have never reached a compromise.

Really serious was my leaving too much of the care of the children to her. Soon after we were married we had some bitter arguments about my handling of Michael. He was a hyperactive child and Martha wanted me to be firm and consistent with him, but frequently she thought me too firm. She herself was not always consistent, either in ideas or emotional reactions, but always positive and emphatic, whatever her position at the moment. I used to say her motto was "nothing in moderation," and her friends thought that fitted. She occasionally said the husband should be dominant in a marriage, a carryover from her early upbringing, but she was careful never to be caught in any such position.

Her psychoanalyst had left her with guilt feelings; she believed that her former unstable marriage had damaged Michael. This led to indulgence on her part and confusion on his. It was aggravated by Mike's father, Bill McCleery, who worked at convincing Mike that his mother had married an insensitive clod of a farmer who could not understand him. This sort of friction encouraged me, unwisely but for the sake of peace, to leave too many of the decisions about the children to Martha. I was a man at mid-life, forty-three years old when we married, with a new family, new obligations, and involvement in a new career, but in fairness to Martha I must say that I should have carried more of the responsibility for the children.

Money had always played very different parts in our lives, and we had very different attitudes about its social value and practical uses. She herself had mixed feelings: she wanted the security it gave her even though she had recoiled from the materialism of her family. Her political enlightenment in college increased that ambivalence. One consequence was that she sometimes came to believe that people she had helped were exploiting her. Her money served as a buffer between her and the world; but she might have been happier if she had been forced to make her way on her talents and character.

I certainly welcomed the prospect of having a financially independent wife. It did not occur to me that this might cost me some of my own independence, even while it freed me to do some of the things I wanted to do with the farm. As a designer I needed only my skills and a pencil. As a farmer there was another requirement, capital. It took me a while to realize that hard work would not by itself produce that.

Martha took for granted that we would have a standard of living which she knew I could not support. It obviously gave her great satisfaction to be able to afford this. Inevitably, I sometimes thought her extravagant, that she offended my ideas about consumption and waste. In a sense, however, my long indifference to money left me in no position to suddenly elevate spending it, or not spending it, to a matter of principle. Also, I could hardly object to her giving our children advantages which I myself could not afford. I had always managed to provide for Maria and myself. When my family suddenly grew, the reality was that Martha was able and willing to do more than her share, and I let her do it.

Life at the farm was strenuous, and Martha pitched in with enthusiasm. She taught herself to cook and soon became an expert. She took care of the flower garden and helped me with the vegetables, sorted and packed apples, and even drove a tractor when needed. For someone who had done very little physical work, her energy and stamina were amazing. She also took part in town projects, the first of them related to the schools. Bethel people welcomed her. They had witnessed incidents caused by Jane's addiction to alcohol, which to them was a moral weakness, and they were relieved to see that I now had a more suitable wife.

When we opened the new farm market in 1951 her personality helped to establish the atmosphere of the place. Her hardest job, however, was the care and feeding of apple pickers, the travail of which is described later in this memoir.

In 1950 and 1951 we had parties at bloom time for our friends. When these became unwieldy, the local PTA, of which Martha was president, used the event to raise money for providing hot lunches in the school. At that time serving hot food to children was thought to be extravagant and somehow subversive. The Apple Blossom Festival soon outgrew the resources of the PTA, and we organized a town-wide association to run it. We had hayrides around the farm, a variety of games played with homemade apparatus, lots of food, and a place for people of all ages to meet their friends. At its height we attracted four to five thousand people in a single afternoon and raised several thousand dollars for public health and recreation projects. After twenty-eight years it was suspended and then abolished. While it existed, it was a fondly remembered experience for generations of local people and incidentally brought tremendous publicity and goodwill to our farm.

There was a one-room school near us, the eight grades taught by a woman who presided there for forty years and whose pupils more than held their own when they got to high school. Three of our children went there at various times. Bethel was in many ways still a nineteenth-century town, with a few summer people from the cities, a majority of longtime residents, and some newcomers. The phenomenal postwar mobility of middle-class people, which was to change the whole social structure of Bethel, had not yet begun.

We had old friends in western Connecticut and made some new ones. The Calders and Millers had preceded me and were living in Roxbury. Malcolm and Muriel Cowley, Matthew and Hannah Josephson, and several other writers and painters had settled in Sherman. They were mostly transplanted New Yorkers, but we soon became acquainted with other families who had been in Con-

With Martha, about 1950

necticut for generations, people in agriculture, the law, manufacturing, and politics.

Martha and I did some traveling. We went to England in 1959 when Maria's husband was studying biostatistics at the University of London and went about the country with them and to Amsterdam for a few days. Another year we went to France, visited the Calders at their place in Saché on the Loire, and toured the chateaux and cathedrals of central France. We took two fine trips west, the first up the Pacific Coast, the Cascade Mountains, and the Olympic Peninsula, the second up the Rockies from Denver into Canada. After Christina's wedding in Tucson, we drove, with Ellen, through Arizona to the Grand Canyon.

When the children no longer needed Martha's attention she did travel without me, with Maria, Cleo and Jim Fitch, and others, and once on an organized tour to Japan. When I think back to how much we enjoyed our few trips together, how much those shared experiences added to our life, I realize how insensitive I was not to take more time away from the farm. This absorption in my work may have seemed necessary at the time; I now see it as one of my greatest mistakes.

Martha had always wanted us to be the center of a close nuclear family, with a large contingent of grandchildren, but it did not work out that way. Maria, who became as much Martha's child as mine, was an independent citizen even before she graduated from Sarah Lawrence College. Art was her major area of study, but she minored in politics. She was hired to do research work in Washington, D.C., for a House committee headed by James Roosevelt. When the project ran out of funds she applied for unemployment insurance and said she knew all about printing, trading on what she got from her father by osmosis. Starting in a small printing office, she eventually became an accomplished typographic designer.

Maria married a Chicago physician named Harold Schoolman who was doing research in hematology. Later they moved to Washington where Harold, known as Hack, ended up at the National Institutes of Health. Maria continued as typographer, painter, and sculptor. They have two bright and humorous children, one of whom delighted me recently by getting a job at the Environmental Protection Agency. The Schoolmans are avid gardeners and live on the most densely planted half acre in the whole District of Columbia.

Michael McCleery is the only one of our children who lives in Connecticut. He was volatile and rebellious, bounced in and out of half a dozen schools, and went to Boston University for a few months. An editor friend found him a job on the *New York Post*; then, disillusioned with the city life he had chosen, he came back to Bethel. Soon he was a reporter on the *Danbury News-Times* and later on the *New Haven Register*. Finally he became a partner in a flourishing small advertising agency, where he makes good use of his creative imagination and humor.

He was married for sixteen years to Nancy O'Connor, a college English teacher and a devout Catholic. They raised two quick-witted sons, one like his mother, one like his father, and also a boy from Nancy's earlier marriage. Mike has been an excellent father to them all. Mike's second marriage, however, seems better suited to the man he became in maturity.

Christina, who calls herself Dallas, had a troubled childhood. When very young she expressed with remarkable drawings the intense fantasy of her inner life. As she matured she proved to be courageous and strong-willed, independent but affectionate, and she treats her life with humor and understanding. She went to art schools in Boston and in Mexico, where somehow this New England girl feels most at home. She crossed the border to Arizona and was married for five years to a young Tucson man named Glenn Erickson. Then she went to the University of Arizona and became an expert at architectural drafting. Still devoted to warm weather and the sea, she now lives and works in St. Petersburg, Florida.

Ellen, our youngest child, inherited her mother's striking good looks. As a child her chief medium of expression was dancing; she improvised delightful routines to entertain us. After eight years in Bethel schools she resisted going to boarding school for a more rounded education, but she finally agreed. She went to Antioch College in Ohio, then, like so many of her generation, quit during her sophomore year. She followed several typical California enthusiasms with a serious interest in the restoration of antique carpets, became skilled at the craft, and studied for a season in London. She has developed other skills, is patient, curious, and disciplined. Her most recent work is in the tourist industry, where she can be paid for traveling about and seeing the world, but her home base is still San Francisco.

The dispersal of her children has been a great disappointment for Martha. Strong personal feelings persist, but distance makes communication difficult. Her devotion and strength of character, much more significant than her inconsistencies, brought her children through many crises, and that is truly recognized. I once gave her a brooch made of three intertwined rings which I said represented work, love, and battle. That seemed to both of us an apt symbol of our life—certainly of the first half of our marriage.

As the children grew older and less dependent on Martha, she became restless. I was so preoccupied with my work that I was surprised when she began to look for ways of escaping the routine of our life. At the height of one harvest season she committed herself to a part-time job assisting Mary Steiner, a photojournalist friend. In 1969 she visited the Hansens in Key West, Florida, and when she returned she told me she had invested in a cottage there. She spent four winters in Key West. It was at this time that we did some traveling to Europe and to the mountains of the Far West. These were rewarding experiences; I did not realize until later how much of Martha's enjoyment of them came from getting me away from the farm.

By the time we had been married for twenty years, Martha and I were no longer meeting each other's physical needs. Differences in background, interests, and habits, overlooked when we were younger, became more significant as we became less absorbed in the lives of our maturing children. She began to feel that marriage to me had not compensated for her early trials and disappointments, and her enthusiasm for farm activities was cooling. Our occasional travels, when we were closer than at home, only emphasized the divisions in our daily life. I was in my sixties and beginning to feel old, not physically, not in my capacity for work, but in spirit.

At that time I developed a deep emotional attachment for a very young woman which lasted for several years. It is difficult to explain what I could find in common with so young a person, but our bond was much more than physical. Knowing her was a rejuvenating experience, far beyond what I might have anticipated. Of course I had no illusions that Martha would be sympathetic or even tolerant. She was bitter and resentful and came to believe that the life we had shared for so many years had been a mistake from the day of our wedding.

By 1976 Martha felt she could no longer live with me, and she moved to a condominium retirement community called Heritage Village in Southbury, some twenty minutes away from the farm. Heritage Village is a well-designed, comfortable community. Martha had friends there and has made many more. During her years there she has followed her lifelong interest in and knowledge of other people's painting by studying and painting herself, producing a body of excellent oils and watercolors admired by her friends and exhibited now and then. We are all proud of her.

I had no reason to think our separation in 1976 would not be permanent. I could not pretend that she had no justification. I can

Martha, about 1958

only regret now that we did not try for a reconciliation, but it did seem to me that patched-up relationships seldom hold their patches and that I would have to face, in my seventies, a repetition of the single life I had lived for nine years before we were married.

At a party in Newtown the following year I encountered a woman I had known slightly for some time. Lillian Hull was divorced from a man I knew from his participation in Bethel affairs. Born on an Ohio farm, she had raised three children, worked as a nurse, and returned to college for a master's degree in clinical psychology. Her patients have included children, the elderly, and the retarded. She is one of the most intuitive and understanding people I have ever known, which is why she is so good at her job. She also has a fine talent for gardening and surplus energy for work like painting her house.

We gradually became close and confidential friends. She has been supportive and tolerant, accepting me with all my other ties and obligations, and for many years we were dependent on one another in many ways. Later, when I was finally enjoying much better relations with Martha, the situation became difficult, and Lillian decided to end our intimacy. Though we now only talk occasionally, we communicate as well as ever.

Neither Martha nor I has at any time contemplated divorce. That would have marked the end of our family solidarity and forced our children to take sides in a family schism. I have not forgotten the obligation I assumed when I married Martha, to try to compensate for the early collapse of her family and later the loss of two children, nor could I ignore her devotion to our own two children and to Maria.

Now, late in our lives, I feel closer to her than I ever have. This increased affection and mutual dependency have brought our children closer too, in spite of geographical separation. This is a tremendous source of pleasure and satisfaction for all of us.

11 🍎 *People and Politics*

When I bought Elizabeth Weed's run-down farm in 1934 and planted my first orchard I did not anticipate that I would spend fifty years in agriculture. For a long time my life was a four-ball juggling act balancing my clients, the Guild, Maria, and the farm. I was designing a great many books, my only source of income. I was spending part of nearly every day helping to run the Book and Magazine Guild. Maria was a constant responsibility. When she was in my care and attending the Hunter school I had a room for her in my studio apartment. When she was staying with Jane I had to be available for crises. All this meant many days in New York and occasionally in other cities where I had publisher clients. Weekends, and whatever other time I could manage, I spent working at the farm.

Bethel was indeed, as I had hoped, not like Weston, less than twenty miles away. The Fairfield County towns bordering Long Island Sound from Greenwich to Fairfield were different. Many of the people there were oriented toward New York; thousands of them worked there. The commuters were by no means a majority, but they included many writers, journalists, entertainers, and advertising professionals. With their access to the media they were able to give the rest of the state the impression that they *were* Fairfield County. They took little part in Connecticut political or cultural life; Yale and Wesleyan and Trinity might as well have been in Massachusetts. They had no links to the huge insurance and manufacturing industries. To them Bethel was certainly an unsophisticated place, but I had seen enough of their kind of sophistication.

Bethel had been part of Danbury until 1855 and was still joined to it economically and socially. Until well after World War II the area did not share the prosperity of most of industrial Connecticut. Its chief product was fur felt hats. The hatters' strike in 1902 was a landmark in labor history. Their union was defeated, and, under the antitrust laws then existing, the Supreme Court in 1908 held the workers liable for the owners' losses. Many of them were bankrupted, and the union was destroyed.

The New York–based Hat, Cap, and Millinery Workers Union assumed jurisdiction, but the officials, many of them European-born socialists, had little stomach for organizing crusty Yankees. They left Dennis (Dinny) Carroll, member of an influential Bethel family, in sole charge, and hatting became mostly an open-shop industry.

Danbury was a one-industry town, and the owners were organized to keep it that way and to keep their shops as the only source of jobs. When war came, the factories could not be converted to munitions production and were shut down. People found there was lots of work in other towns and learned to commute, and the manufacturers' control of labor ended. Hat wearing went out of style after the war, and the effort to keep out other industries was reversed. New enterprises were drawn into the vacuum, and people with technical or managerial skills came with them. They changed Bethel from a country town into a suburb. Twenty years after the war, 70 percent of Bethel's residents were working in other towns. Developers became active, notably the Steiner brothers from Monroe who built hundreds of houses in the north part of town on land not suitable for farming.

In the eastern part, where my farm was, and in the southern part there were many small subsistence farms whose owners worked part-time in factories or in construction. Farmers' methods and, in many cases, personalities had changed very little since the nineteenth century. Getting to know these people gave me a feeling for America's rural past which I could not have experienced a few years later. This stayed with me through my fifty years of farming and, as I can see in retrospect, influenced my approach to twentieth-century problems. Many of my neighbors were from old Bethel families, as I expected, but a number had other, sometimes surprising, backgrounds.

Elizabeth Weed, whose farm I bought, came to Bethel in the 1890s to be Henry Weed's housekeeper after the death of his wife, Hattie Bell. Following a not uncommon practice, he married her to save wages. He died four years before I arrived, after several years in the Newtown mental hospital. Elizabeth supported herself by keeping summer boarders, young city couples who enjoyed the romance of poor food and no plumbing or who could not afford anything better.

Henry Weed, sometimes referred to as Old Pink Whiskers, was dead, but his eccentricities survived. We found that he had sold an unused right-of-way across the farm for twenty-five dollars, but had never told his wife or shared the money with her. His barn was built with a hip roof, meant to be supported by triangular trusses which leave the barn's interior free of the usual posts and beams. Henry liked the up-to-date look of the hip roof, but he had no confidence in any newfangled trusses, so the barn still had post-and-beam framing.

George Edmond's family was one of the oldest in the county. He had a few cows whose milk we bought until they were condemned by the state for carrying a bovine disease. When he no longer had livestock to graze his rocky pastures, he mowed his fields by hand every year until his death at seventy-eight. No self-respecting farmer would have brush growing in the fields. He never owned a tractor. He was one of three elected assessors, a routine job until the large acreage of overlooked and underassessed land led the town to hire a professional.

Gertrude Edmond, George's widow, sold me their land after George died in 1965. She lived alone for many years on the proceeds, refusing her two daughters' offers to take care of her. Her great pleasures were her demitasse collection and the braided rugs she made.

Everett Havens, my nearest neighbor, became my best friend in Bethel. He was a very skillful farmer, and I learned a lot from him. He grew up in a fertile area near Riverhead, Long Island. He fell in love with a vacationing New York City girl, which was not what his family expected or wanted. After their wedding they ferried across Long Island Sound with all their possessions on a horse-drawn wagon and proceeded inland to Bethel. Everett first rented a farm, then bought the one adjoining mine. He grew the same crops he had known as a boy, chiefly potatoes, cauliflower, strawberries, and asparagus. After I planted my first orchard he ventured to plant one of his own. Hand-hoeing his vegetables, he accumulated hundreds of arrowheads. He feared his crops were being stolen, and one cold fall night he asked me to help investigate. We went out with our shotguns and caught a man in the cauliflower patch. I had to hold him there until Everett located our one police officer.

Lillian Havens, Everett's hardworking wife, packaged asparagus and other vegetables, sorted potatoes, tended hens, and boxed eggs. She and Gertrude Edmond were friends, as neighbors had to be, but she was envious of the Edmonds' status and perhaps self-conscious about her city accent and was privately critical. Everett and George seemed oblivious to this. Lillian kept tabs on her neighbors with binoculars. One day she told me, "I saw your cat follow you out back."

The Rockwell family farm on nearby Rockwell Road was divided by four brothers. Frank, the oldest, kept most of the land and farmed it until he was too old. His brothers were carpenters. Paul, the youngest, was the first man in Bethel to call me by my first name. He had a beautiful wife who ran away—to Texas it was said. Frank's wife, Anna, taught all her life at the one-room Plumtrees School. Three of my children were her pupils at various times.

David Judd, part of one of the most influential old Bethel families, had his house and barns on the edge of town. He drove his herd to and from his pasture half a mile out on Plumtrees Road. If you were catching a train, as I often was, you had to remember those cows. Dave sold machinery, and I bought my first second-hand tractor and harrow from him for $200.

Jackson Cooper was an actor of the silent screen. When sound came to pictures he retired to the small farm adjoining mine to the north. He brought no aura of Hollywood with him, and there was nothing to distinguish him from any other farmer. His land was mostly gravel with a thin layer of topsoil, and he did not do very well there. A few years after I arrived he sold out to Louise Munn.

Louise Munn was a young woman who loved horses. She had

a wealthy admirer who was never visible, but we thought we knew his name. He bought the Cooper place for Louise; she rebuilt the house and stables and enjoyed her horses and his discreet visits. This introduced a bit of spice to the Plumtrees district. When she lost her friend's support she lived on sales of gravel, then sold out to a contractor and disappeared.

The Merrill farm adjoined the Rockwells'. By 1934 Mr. Merrill was dead and his widow was keeping boarders in the large house and converted outbuildings. Then she sold the place to a famous opera singer named Queena Mario, who conducted a school there. In warm weather we could hear her students' voices carry half a mile on the breeze. Ethel Barrimore Colt, who had been a theater friend of my wife Jane, studied there.

Elmer Allison was a Bethel farmer unique because he had connections with New York radicals. How that happened I never heard. He married a New Yorker, and she became a conspicuously outspoken but well-liked Bethel citizen. She was one of the few people in town who had any knowledge of my past history.

Sometimes I would go to the farm alone to work and then into Danbury for supplies and a good dinner at a restaurant patronized by railroad men. I met Art Young there. He had lived quietly in Bethel for many years, and few people knew that he was a cartoonist and humorist famous nationally for his contributions to radical magazines. When I knew him his wife was dead; no longer able to provide for himself, he was living in a Danbury boardinghouse. He spent his days walking on Main Street, talking to anyone with time to listen to his great stories.

The Underhills had a farm near me on Old Hawleyville Road. In the forties they sold it to a Bridgeport man who, with his brothers, controlled the American branch of the Canadian McKesson and Robbins liquor and chemical business. His brothers' last name was Musica, but he took an assumed name which I cannot recall and which does not appear in any public records, so he can only be called Mr. X. An ostentatious Masonic official, he bought the farm to provide a cemetery for his fellow lodge members. Roads and a winter vault were built, but no one was ever buried there.

The three brothers were found to be embezzling company funds, and Mr. X committed suicide. The cemetery had never been given to the Masons; it was still held in his name. The bankruptcy court sold it to people who proposed building a crematory. This enraged the neighbors, who feared that an odor of burning bodies would taint the country air. After a series of sales and resales the land became the Vining Road housing development.

My neighbors were naturally curious about the urban newcomer who landed in their midst with plans to farm. I certainly could not pretend to know much about farming, but I found them friendly and cooperative from the beginning. I spent my first year making the place habitable for my wife and infant daughter. With a little help, I built an addition to the old house, with a kitchen and pantry downstairs and a bedroom and bath above. I used mostly secondhand lumber and plumbing fixtures. In those depression days there was a flourishing trade in salvaging material from old houses, cleaning and sorting it and selling it to thrifty people like me. When I finished work on the house and promptly planted a good-sized orchard, the neighbors could see that I was serious and accepted me.

There was a one-room school nearby, the last one in Bethel and eventually one of the last in Connecticut, and a Plumtrees School Association existed to help support it. Social activities were part of the program, and I was asked to lend my barn for dances. Mine was the only farm without livestock; I sold my hay in the field, and the barn was empty. For a couple of years the association held dances there. These were square dances, the kind my neighbors, many of them elderly, had grown up with and enjoyed without the self-consciousness and cute costumes of later country-dance enthusiasts. Unfortunately, my barn had not been well constructed, and it was not as sturdy as it looked. The weight and rhythm of the dancers shook the building and split a few timbers. The dances were abolished lest a huge collapse wipe out half the neighborhood.

About four thousand people lived in Bethel in 1935; there were over four times that number by the 1980s. Most of the older houses were built in the nineteenth century; some of the very old ones had been altered to meet Victorian tastes. Two of the more prosperous residents had summer cottages on streams no more than three miles from the center of town.

There were four established churches when I came to Bethel: Congregational, Methodist, Episcopal, and Roman Catholic. The town was founded when a Congregational group separated from their Danbury parish. By the 1930s the Catholics in Bethel equaled or exceeded the total number of Protestants. I found the social and political influence of the Catholics, as it changed during my long residence in the town, a fascinating study. At first Yankee Protestant Republican families controlled the town as they always had in most of New England, and the Democrats, although mostly Irish Catholics, were careful to keep some Protestant names on their election slates.

The Democrats were always prolabor and identified themselves with the working class, but they were not otherwise conspicuously liberal. Gradually changes in the outlook of the Catholic church, the influence of Vatican II, intermarriage with Protestants, and finally the leadership of liberal Catholic New Dealers placed local Democrats firmly on the side of social progress. Election tickets balanced by church affiliation became a thing of the past.

There were few Jews in Bethel, no synagogue, and no visible anti-Jewish feeling. During the years when I belonged to the Lions Club, the largest and oldest service club in town, we had two Jewish presidents. There were very few nonwhite people and no "Negro" neighborhood. The largest garage was owned by Bill Reilly, a black man, and there were few signs of discrimination. Some venal realtors promoted the idea that black ownership lowered nearby real-estate values, but that was largely ignored. In Danbury, only three miles away, there was an influx of Southern blacks after World War II. They finally made up 10 percent of the population, one of the important communities in a heterogeneous small city.

Before World War II most people thought that antifascists were all radicals. A few years later our leading antifascist was the president of the United States, and most Americans were supporting him. I would like to believe that we early radicals had awakened the majority of people to the Fascist menace, but in fact, as we now know, even Roosevelt could not bring us into the war until the Japanese settled the issue for us at Pearl Harbor.

I had wanted to make Bethel my hometown from the day I bought the farm, but because of my other responsibilities it took me ten years to do it. My first participation in town affairs was in 1944 when I went to the Democratic party caucus. I knew there were not many Democrats in Bethel, but I was surprised to find only thirteen people at the meeting, which was called to nominate a candidate for the lower house of the state legislature. After a long delay, I was asked to be that candidate. "Why do you want me?" I asked. "We'd like a new face on the ticket." "How much work would I have to do?" "Oh, don't worry, you won't be elected." "I mean how much campaign work?" "Oh, we don't do much campaigning, but you can do some for yourself, if you like." So I became a name at the bottom of the Democratic ticket, headed at the top by Franklin D. Roosevelt, who was running for his fourth term in the White House.

My campaign consisted of a few newspaper ads devoted chiefly to criticisms of Thomas Dewey, candidate for president, and of Claire Booth Luce, who was running for reelection to Congress. I spent some time working for Luce's opponent, Margaret Connors, who nearly won in the strongly Republican Fourth Congressional District. I also joined the Bethel Democratic committee, and after a year or two of showing more zeal and optimism than most of my fellow members, I was elected chairman.

With that responsibility, I tried to shake up the party. I made an attempt, ultimately unsuccessful, to drop Edgar Platt, our perennial candidate for first selectman (our top executive). He was an amiable man, related by marriage to several of the Republican leaders, and his political credo was, "I don't like to step on anybody's toes." On the whole, my short tenure as chairman, while it improved the standing of the Democrats in Bethel, was not welcomed by party insiders. They were quite comfortable with the party's minority status and the small official plums that state statutes gave to the minority party without the need for any political exertion. They were obviously relieved when I resigned in 1948 to work for the election of Henry Wallace on a third-party ticket.

Wallace was living on a farm in South Salem, New York, fifteen miles west of Bethel. He had resumed his agricultural experiments there after he resigned from Harry Truman's cabinet in 1946. I first became acquainted with him at a dinner in Brookfield, and he came to parties at my house several times. He had been a farm journalist and plant breeder in Iowa, then Roosevelt's secretary of agriculture and vice president. He was a trusted friend of FDR, an able administrator, and a combative politician, with a vision of social justice and world peace. Many Democrats thought him the best-equipped person to carry on Roosevelt's New Deal.

He was too liberal, however, for powerful party conservatives, and they persuaded FDR not to support him for renomination as vice president in 1944.

He became secretary of commerce, and after Roosevelt's death in 1945 he was an outspoken opponent of President Truman's Cold War program. He criticized Truman's foreign policy at huge meetings of people alarmed by prospects of war, policies which led only a few years later to our intervention in Korea and after that in Vietnam. Truman asked him to leave the cabinet. There were influential voices calling for a third party, but Wallace still hoped to move the Democrats to his own progressive position. By the end of 1947 he gave up that hope and agreed to head a new party, the Progressive party.

Although I wanted to help make the Democrats a force for progress in Bethel, I became increasingly troubled by the policies of Truman and the national party. I felt Roosevelt's principles were being abandoned and that the nation was being led into another war. When a new party to support Henry Wallace was organized in Connecticut, I resigned my Bethel chairmanship and joined it. Martha found that people she had known years before in the civil rights movement were among Wallace's advisors, and she backed the new party with enthusiasm.

The new party's support in the Fourth Congressional District was weak. We lacked the solid liberal base provided elsewhere by academics at Yale and other institutions, and the district was dominated by the wealthy, largely Republican towns of the so-called gold coast.

As a farmer, a former Democratic town chairman, and a one-time union official, I qualified as a suitable party figure. I became one of five vice-chairmen of the state party and later was nominated for the Fourth District seat in Congress. I made speeches at meetings around the state, presided once at a huge rally in the Bushnell auditorium in Hartford, and did some house-to-house canvassing in Bethel. It was our policy, however, not to oppose any Democrat who had labor support, and before the election I withdrew from the ticket in favor of William Gaston, who had been endorsed for Congress by a number of unions.

The Progressive party was the legal name of some old forgotten Connecticut organization, so we took the name People's party. We were joined by many Democrats with long histories of loyal party activity, under the chairmanship of Charles Calkins, who had been administrative assistant to Democratic senator Brian McMahon. Calkins died on the eve of our first convention; Thomas I. Emerson, an eminent Yale law professor, succeeded him and was nominated for governor.

Harry Truman was nominated for president by the Democrats, but he was less than popular, and many Democrats wanted Dwight Eisenhower, whose party affiliation was still uncertain. The Republican candidate was Tom Dewey again; the press and the polls predicted that he would win easily. Truman clearly needed the votes that might go to Wallace, and his campaign was chiefly devoted to cutting down Wallace's support. This was done by attacking Wallace's patriotism and calling him a puppet of the communists.

Wallace had been saying for years that Truman's policies would lead to war, that the United States should build on the victories of World War II by economic and political cooperation with the Soviet Union, and that the Soviets, after losing over twenty million men in defeating the Nazi invasion, were in no position to fight again. The Truman campaign accused Wallace of being pro-Soviet and anti-American. This was made easier for them because Wallace refused to reject the support of the tiny American Communist party, which agreed with his peace policies and worked for his election.

Red-baiting dominated the campaign. Many anti-Soviet liberals joined in attacking Wallace, and the press was united in whipping up the hysteria. Typical of the absurd effort to express their hatred was an editorial in the *Danbury News-Times* which called Wallace "a ruthless dreamer." The Democrats were right to fear that a successful Wallace campaign could result in Truman's defeat. In spite of Dewey's complacency, Truman finally won by only two million votes; Wallace received a million. Strom Thurmond, candidate of a fourth party of Southern Democrats who thought Truman too liberal, got three-quarters of a million. There were 12,700 votes for Wallace in Connecticut, 25 of them in Bethel.

Red-baiting had proved to be a successful political tactic. It showed Senator Joe McCarthy how much mileage there was in it and encouraged him to carry on his shameless rampage for years, with the tacit approval of many respectable and powerful people. It penetrated to every level of public life. In 1952 the Republicans in my own town accused the Democrats of "crime, corruption, and communism," of dealing in "life blood, youth, and humanity." Can there be any doubt that this kind of mindless rhetoric owed its origin to the Truman and McCarthy campaigns?

Wallace tried to keep the third party alive after the 1948 defeat, but it was increasingly dominated by the left-wingers. They had supported the Wallace program loyally and worked hard for its success, but now they wanted more control of the party's agenda. In 1950, when the United States became involved in the Korean civil war, the national committee of the Progressive party drafted a statement condemning our intervention. Wallace opposed that statement, as did a minority of the committee. He said that he had warned against such entanglements, but when the United States was actually at war he would support his country. That rift ended his connection with the Progressive party and his hopes for saving humanity from its follies.

Henry Wallace failed as a practical politician, but his speeches were sound and prophetic, and time has proven him to be right. Richard J. Walton wrote in his 1976 book, *Henry Wallace, Harry Truman, and the Cold War*: "Henry Wallace was essentially right and Harry Truman was essentially and tragically wrong. Henry Wallace said that the United States could not purchase reliable friends. He said that the United States would end up supporting corrupt, incompetent, and repressive dictators all over the world. He said that the United States would not be able to stamp out revolution the world over. He said that the effort to contain communism would be costly in American blood and treasure. He said that a crusade against communism would lead to the repression of civil liberties at home. He said that American foreign policy would lead to militarism. He said that the Truman Doctrine, the Marshall Plan, and NATO would divide the world into hostile camps. He said that Truman's foreign policy would cause the colonial peoples of the world to identify Russia and communism as their friends and the United States as their enemy. He said, in short, that Harry Truman's foreign policy would lead to disaster at home and abroad. Henry Wallace was right."

I like to think of Henry Wallace as I often see him in a large photograph at the Agricultural Experiment Station in New Haven. It was taken with two of the station scientists, when he was working with them on corn-breeding experiments that enriched the world. It reminds me of the Wallace whose deep roots in agriculture led so naturally to his concern for all humanity's problems. It reminds me of his courage in leaving the farm and the laboratory to fight for his beliefs in the political arena. His was a career I would have liked to emulate, had I his talents and opportunities.

I did not regret my decision to join the Wallace movement, but I was naturally not welcomed back into Bethel political circles for some years. I remained a registered Democrat but with so little ability to influence party policy in Bethel that I qualified as an Independent Democrat; perhaps "Impotent Democrat" was the more realistic term. Further tries for public office were out of the question, but in any case I knew that I was what is called a controversial personality, the sort of candidate that politicians try to avoid.

My joining the Wallace movement did not seem to affect my standing in the town, perhaps because what happened inside the Democratic party did not seem of much importance to most Bethel people. For the next thirty years I was active first in Bethel town affairs and then in state politics. I was elected to serve as moderator at many town meetings. At some of these the discussion of such topics as the town budget became unruly, and my experience in the chair during my union days was useful.

The first public mention of the Wallace affair came nine years later, in 1957, when I was a leader of the bipartisan Bethel Good Government League. The League stung members of both parties with accusations of inefficient government, occasional corruption, and constant interparty collaboration. At that time Governor Abraham Ribicoff appointed me to the State Board of Agriculture. The Bethel Democrats published an open letter to him protesting his appointing me without consulting them and saying that I had been disloyal to the party in 1948 and had joined a "Communist-dominated" campaign. Ribicoff ignored the letter, and I served on that board for twenty-two years. As this incident suggests, working for Wallace was not looked on everywhere as an unforgivable political crime.

The upheaval in Connecticut people's working habits during and after World War II hit Danbury and Bethel with exaggerated impact. The demise of hatting and the coming of new industries and people with new skills changed the social structure of the two towns. Many of these were women joining the work force for the first time. People were losing their roots, their sense of identity as members of a stable group and as citizens of a given place. Cultural changes were accelerated by the universal ownership of automobiles and by the success of mercantile interests in fostering the growth of a goods-oriented society. This perceived need for what was euphemistically called a high standard of living was making people vulnerable to demagogic claims that they could not "afford" the costs of good schools and efficient government.

The impact on Bethel was striking. The town meeting, which was effective when people knew and trusted their neighbors, lost its traditional democratic character. Politics as we had known it was not working. There was increased resistance to paying the taxes needed to support schools and services, even while there was a growing demand for public recreation facilities. There was organized opposition to new ways of dealing with rapid growth, such as municipal planning and zoning. Dominated for a hundred years by the Republicans, Bethel was suffering from the familiar results of one-party government: neglect of serious public issues, occasional illegal actions, and the frequent election of incompetent officials.

At that time our first selectman was usually a retired hatter with good family connections but little education and no experience in government. I remember a characteristic speech by one of these Republican leaders, Louis Shaw, at a dinner for the retiring postmaster. He said, "Whoever our next postmaster may be, he will never wear, in the hearts of the people, the shoes that Frank Hurgin has worn." This was funny enough to remember but not very amusing as a measure of the mentality of the man who was in charge of Bethel's government, roads, social services, and public health and safety.

In 1955, in an effort to find out whether we could escape from a series of Louis Shaws, I sent a questionnaire to eighteen towns of our size asking how much their first selectman was paid and what duties were performed. The replies showed that we were paying a top salary in Bethel and receiving a minimum of service. I circulated this information, and it led to the formation of the Bethel Good Government League, a bipartisan group of over a hundred citizens. In three years of existence we were able to get action on many neglected local problems. This so upset the town power structure that at one point the Democrats and Republicans were each accusing the other party of controlling the league. As usual, I was identified as the chief troublemaker.

I found many opportunities for useful activity outside of partisan politics. The daily *Danbury News-Times* was controlled by the owner of the largest hat factory. It was flagrantly anti-union, opposed to needed welfare proposals, and devoted to keeping out new industry. In 1948 I joined two Danbury lawyers in making plans for an independent paper. We were assured of financial backing, but we abandoned the project when we were convinced that business leaders and church people, supporters of the status quo, would make it impossible to maintain the necessary corps of boys to deliver our paper to Danbury and Bethel homes. Fortunately the *News-Times* was sold a few years later to the owners of a newspaper chain, who ran it in a professional manner without slanted reporting and buried stories, and I became friendly with the new editor and several staff members.

I joined a successful effort to establish a planning and zoning commission and served as a member for a while. Life on the commission was stormy and strenuous, but we managed to get public support for orderly town growth under sensible regulations. Discussions of a regional planning agency were not so successful. They were disrupted by people from certain other towns who feared that a regional plan would bring new housing occupied by people from Harlem and others foreign to Fairfield County. The need for cooperation across the borders of Connecticut's 169 small towns was so acute, however, that the selectmen finally used their authority to set up a regional council of elected officials. This functioned as an effective planning body.

In 1948 I was appointed chairman of a committee to find a site for a new school to accommodate hundreds of so-called war babies, the first elementary school to be built in Bethel since 1897. We found a fine site, a mile from the crowded center of town. Some people in Bethel objected; they believed that all children ought to walk to school, but the land was bought and eventually became part of an educational park with five schools. I then became chairman of the building committee and thus the target of a taxpayers' association opposed to the project. They first claimed that the preschool children, already living and counted, did not exist. They then offered spurious figures to prove that our plans were extravagant. Finally they hinted that we were engaged in some kind of radical conspiracy to pick the pockets of the taxpayers. The school proposal was defeated.

The secretary of our building committee was Frank Berry, retired superintendent of schools and a devout Methodist. He had never faced any hostility nor had his integrity ever been questioned, and he died an unhappy man before the school was finally built under the direction of a new committee. It opened in 1952 and was named the Frank A. Berry School. As for me, I survived and was able to take further part in the constant struggles for adequate school facilities and the tax money to operate them.

A few years later there was a proposal to enlarge what was then the Bethel High School. Hilda Walker, chair of the Board of Education, favored enlarging the old building, which was already too big for the land it stood on. I told her that I intended to campaign against her project. Within forty-eight hours she was spreading a false rumor that I wanted to sell some of my land for a new school. Her plan prevailed, and it was later disclosed that she had an interest, as a realtor, in a piece of land that was bought to enlarge the school parking lot.

I had a discussion with a prosperous and much admired Bethel citizen named J. Harry White. He was on the school board and was publicly supporting Walker's proposal, although privately opposed to it. I asked him why he did not speak out openly. "Bob," he said, "you always say what you think, and look what happens to you." "All that happens," I replied, "is that some people don't love me." I could see why everybody loved Harry White.

The Democratic registration in Bethel was growing, due largely to the influx of people brought by the postwar economic revival of the Danbury area. In 1958, for the first time ever, Democrats were elected to represent Bethel in the legislature, and in 1959 David Deakin became the first Democrat to be first selectman. Since then Democrats have usually won most of the local elections, although the town consistently gives majorities to Republican candidates for governor and president. This confirms the theory that people vote for those they know and trust but vote by party affiliation for those remote from their experience.

By the 1970s most of my old party adversaries were no longer active or had forgiven my early defection, and I was asked to rejoin the Democratic Town Committee. Then in 1986 I was nominated for a seat in the State House of Representatives, forty-two years after my first candidacy. This was no great honor; Bethel had become part of a district which included the overwhelmingly Republican town of Brookfield. We had not won the seat in many years, but I felt I should take my turn on the ticket. I was endorsed by Abe Ribicoff and other high-ranking Democrats, but, as expected, I did not win. It was in this campaign that someone in my opponent's camp circulated a rumor that I had once been a member of the Communist party. There was no evidence that anyone paid attention to that or that it affected the vote.

In 1988 I was one of some 250 people at a dinner marking the retirement of former Bethel selectman Dave Deakin, who had served for twenty years as a housing official in Hartford. As usual on such occasions, government and party leaders were introduced by the toastmaster. He called on me to take a bow as "the oldest living liberal Democrat in Connecticut." The toastmaster was Charles McCollam, Jr., then an aide to the governor and a power in the Democratic organization. He was the son of one of my most bitter antagonists of the forties.

12 🍎 *No Gentleman Farmer*

I was very lucky in finding the farm I bought in 1934. The first attraction was the low price, $7,500 for a house with five small rooms and no plumbing on what was described in the town records as "fifty acres more or less." I liked the site; it was on high ground, and the house was set further from the road than most farmhouses and had big trees around it. A mile away was a hollow, known as Plumtrees, with a group of old houses and an ice pond and icehouse. Our road, called Plumtrees Road, led from there up a long hill and past my farm.

Someone asked me years later what it was like to start a whole new life at thirty-one, but I did not think of it as a big change; in fact, it was just another project I was undertaking, as I had undertaken others. It did of course require establishing a new home, but that was not very different from having a part-time second home on the farm in Weston. I did not plan to make farming my chief occupation; I had no conception of how absorbing it could become and how it could lead me into so many related activities.

I bought the place from Elizabeth Weed, who kept a mortgage for $3,000 or $4,000; Ed Norman and the Calders loaned me the rest. I had only enough cash for minimal improvements. Elizabeth Weed had supplied herself and her boarders with water from a well 40 feet from the house. She carried water to her kitchen and threw the slops out the door. The boarders bathed in a cabin built over the well. When the new rooms were finished I had an electric pump installed. The well was shallow and soon went dry, and I had to have a deep well drilled. We struck water at 160 feet, and this still supplies the house. The farm had a large barn only thirty or forty years old and several small rickety sheds. I gradually replaced the sheds with a new garage, a workshop, and a small poultry house, all of which I was able to build with just an occasional helper.

As far as I could tell, novice that I was, the soil was good. A neighbor, Everett Havens, was growing vegetables on two of the fields. I learned that my farm and several adjoining ones were on a drumlin, with soil highly suitable for growing fruits and vegetables. A drumlin, as any geologist will tell you, is a long, gently sloping hill composed of soils left by a melting glacier.

On the west side was a narrow valley, with some swamps and a good clear brook which flowed all year. We built a half-acre pond there for irrigation and swimming. This became a recreation center for children and friends. We also dug a smaller pond in the center of the orchards to collect surface runoff and supply the sprayers and later a third pond for irrigation.

In 1935 I planted 565 trees, alternating apples and peaches in the rows. The peaches would grow faster, bear younger, and complete their shorter life cycle by the time the apples needed extra space. Growing peaches as "filler trees" was a common practice on commercial fruit farms. My land had been neglected for years, except for two fields that my neighbor Havens was renting. It was on those fields of five or six acres that I planted the first orchard.

I planted another orchard every few years after the first one. With the financial help of my second wife, Martha, I bought two adjoining farms and part of a third, and the place I christened Blue Jay Orchards became one of the larger fruit farms in Connecticut. At first I called it Blue J Orchards, a name easier to remember than Josephy, and that evolved into Blue Jay. There were a few jays around, but I was not thinking of that handsome but raucous bird as a mascot. Much of Bethel's land was steep and rocky, its farms neither large nor very productive. Most of them were turned into house lots as the population grew, and Blue Jay became the last farm in the town.

Like many old Connecticut farms, mine was divided into small fields by stone walls and dotted here and there with large boulders, all of which impeded farm operations. I gradually removed most of these, first with the help of my neighbors, their horses, and a flat sledge called a stone boat. Early tractors were crude and inefficient, and farmers who had them still depended on animal power for certain jobs. Years later, when I had a better tractor, we used that. After World War II, when former navy Construction Battalion drivers (CBs or Seabees) with bulldozers were looking for work, I had them dig trenches and bury the stone walls. This saved land, allowed free movement for equipment, and saved the work of cutting brush that would otherwise grow on the walls.

No farm equipment came with the farm. I bought a used disc harrow and an old Fordson tractor from a neighbor. The tractor was Henry Ford's companion to his famous Model T car and was equally primitive. It had iron wheels with big lugs that could either dig the tractor into the ground or make it rear up like a bronco. It was cranked by hand and was famous for breaking farmers' arms.

After a year I bought an ancient sprayer from another neighbor. Its pump was powered by a one-cylinder engine, also hand-cranked. When I went out to spray my main job was cranking; one engine or the other would stall, and often both of them at once. These machines would do for taking care of my young orchard, but by 1940 I needed something better. Fortunately, I inherited a little money and was able to buy a new Oliver tractor and a new John Bean sprayer. They served me well for many years.

At first the trees did not take much of my time. I had a lot of work to do on the house and farm buildings and a large kitchen garden to plant and cultivate. I was producing a great many books for depression-level fees and teaching my design class, so I had to keep a modest studio apartment in the city. The farmhouse, heated only by stoves and with no insulation, was too cold in the winter for a Southern woman with a small child.

Some of my land was not suitable for fruit trees or for any other crop. There was a long stony piece along the east side, with a flowing spring that kept part of it wet. This had been the farm pasture, but by 1934 it was growing up to brush. We could still see pheasant hunters there in the fall, their heads showing above the bushes, but I had no use for such land and it soon became woodland. My neighbors used wood for heating and cooking. Several of them owned woodlots east of us in Newtown, where the old pastures had already grown into forest. Now and then I helped them cut and haul firewood and sawlogs.

Connecticut had a network of railroads before the days of good roads and large trucks. A single-track line, grandly called the Shepaug Litchfield and Northern, came through the main street of Bethel and wound its way past several small limestone quarries to a junction at Hawleyville, where it joined a line from Litchfield. It formed the west boundary between the Weed farm and the Havens'. Built in 1871, it was abandoned in 1908. Later, when I owned land on both sides of the roadbed, there were five-inch trees growing on it. I bought an acre from the New York, New Haven, and Hartford Railroad for $175, a transaction which had to be approved by the trustees and took three years. It became one of the farm roads.

The Shepaug had been well engineered; I acquired a handsome cattle pass built of massive granite blocks to give livestock a safe passage under the tracks. At the edge of Bethel, where the railroad crossed a brook, there is a beautiful granite arched bridge, an architectural treasure still in perfect condition.

I had no trouble deciding what to grow. The old farm orchard of twenty-five or thirty trees was in poor shape, but a little time taking care of it reinforced my decision to produce fruit. Also, I learned that a planting of young trees would not require more time than I could spare from my other responsibilities.

To say that I had to work hard is an understatement, but I enjoyed it. One thing I had not anticipated: I developed a reputation among my neighbors, and presently all over Bethel, for being a hard worker. This went a long way toward getting me accepted in a town where newcomers were suspect, especially a newcomer who did not go to church and had some unusual ideas. I learned that whether I read the same books as my neighbors was irrelevant—how I made my living was the thing that defined me. I should have learned that from reading Karl Marx, but I only learned it by experience.

Hard work was not my main problem, of course. With only a little gardening behind me, I had a lot to learn to be a farmer. I took my first lessons in horticulture from LeRoy Chapman, Fairfield County agent in the Agricultural Extension Service. For years I depended on him for every step I took. Having respect for the complicated techniques of printing, I was wary of proceeding in a new trade without any training or experience. Later I also received help from the fruit specialist at the University of Connecticut, and there were meetings for growers in all the New England states where I could learn and of course plenty of books and pamphlets. I also absorbed a great deal about general farming practices from my neighbors.

New England was hit by a severe hurricane in 1938. It blew off most of my first crop of peaches and tipped over a few hundred young trees that I had planted in 1937. This second orchard was the last I was able to plant until after World War II. I still had heavy responsibilities in New York and needed to spend much of my time there. I had to stretch myself to keep the farm going, but I was happy doing it. Working with soils and plants, I was putting down cultural and spiritual roots for the first time in my life, roots that urban middle-class merchants like my antecedents seldom had, and I was determined not to lose them.

One thing that was not a factor in my urban life as a designer was the weather. I expected that to be a problem on the farm, and it was. Besides the menace of frosts and freezes, the weather affected plant growth, damage by plant pests, the pollination of blossoms, and my ability to take machinery into the orchards in wet seasons. I had suffered my share of frustration with printers whose work was careless and slipshod, and I liked to say that I would rather deal with the cussedness of nature than with the cussedness of man.

When I bought Elizabeth Weed's farm in 1934, I did not deliberately plan to make agriculture my chief occupation. I thought of it first as a way of supplementing my income and as a way of escaping from the city. In a few years, however, as I wrestled with the complicated problems I had undertaken and learned some of the techniques of coping with them, I began to appreciate the challenges and rewards of my new vocation.

Everyone knows the attractions of the out-of-doors. To me the farm also offered a chance to learn what I could in a new and unlimited area of knowledge: in agricultural practice, in agricultural science, in agricultural politics. It offered me the excitement of gambling on weather and markets. It offered me an opening to the community beyond what was available to a free-lance artist and technician attached to an urban industry. It offered me an expanded opportunity to be self-sufficient, to escape further from the service-dependent bourgeois life of my youth, to continue shaping the kind of world I wanted to live in. This was not a romantic idea; I could see that making it happen would depend on producing substantial crops and on making the farm pay.

I was by no means what is called a gentleman farmer; indeed, any person who made the mistake of calling me one was quickly corrected. For years I did all the farm work, except for an occasional job that needed more than one pair of hands. I have always found physical labor immensely satisfying; I always prided myself on knowing that there was no job on the farm that I could not or would not do myself. Of course, being more mortal than I liked to admit, I found when I was much older that even I had physical limitations.

Fortunately, the development of new farm machinery eventually made manual work easier. For example, the vital job of spraying trees had always required handling a spray hose and gun, carrying water and chemicals under 600 to 700 pounds of pressure. For years the spraying was done by me and my most experienced helper, riding down orchard rows on top of the sprayer tank and directing the spray into the trees on either side. By the mid-sixties this strenuous work ended; we had a new type of machine that automatically blew a cloud of mist into the trees. A well-trained driver could control the spray from the tractor seat and do the work formerly done by three of us.

Rotary mowers largely replaced in orchards the old sickle-bar hay mower, which was slower, needed more skill to operate, and seemed always in need of repairs. Pneumatic or hydraulic-powered pruning shears took most of the muscle work out of one of the major orchard jobs and enabled a person to trim more trees in a day with less fatigue.

There was some work I did because I had the skills, such as the carpentry jobs constantly needed to repair and improve buildings and market facilities. This I always enjoyed. There was other work I did by choice, such as planting and hoeing vegetables and young trees. The emotional satisfaction of direct contact with the earth is no myth; it is one of the rewards of the farmer and the gardener.

Any freshly turned soil, whether from a farmer's hoe or the steels of a huge tractor-drawn cultivator, has a color and texture and even an odor that cannot long survive the onslaught of wind and rain or the tread of humans and animals. Its purity awaits only the farmer's plan for adding to its fertility, for conducting water and nutrients to the seeds that will be sown in it, and for using it to give physical support to the small plants those seeds will produce. That is what soil is for. It has nourished plants and animals since long before the culture called agriculture taught people how to use it. The key word is "use"; efforts to preserve the beauty of untouched virgin soil have never been able to compete with humanity's other needs.

There were many farm jobs I did not particularly enjoy: grading and packing fruit, making cider, tending a cash register on busy days at our market, calling wholesale customers for orders, buying supplies, keeping records and accounts, and in the early days delivering apples to stores and to retail customers' homes.

As Fairfield County became more and more urbanized I sometimes felt like an anachronism. A few people obviously thought there was something a little quaint and out-of-date about farming for a living or seemed to think it was some sort of expensive hobby. By that time we had a flourishing retail farm market. One Sunday I was working there, the place was full of customers, and I thought we looked as if we were doing all right. A rather overdressed country gentleman–type asked me if I was the owner and did I perhaps want a partner. "Why?" I asked. "Well," he said, "I'm looking for some kind of investment that will give me a tax loss."

When I bought the farm I of course knew that I would need fertile, well-drained soil to grow good trees and fruit. Fortunately, I had that. All open land cannot be farmed efficiently; only 7 percent of the earth's surface land can grow crops. In the forty-eight contiguous American states, however, nearly half of the land can be cultivated, which is how this nation first became rich and powerful. Connecticut has some of the nation's best soil. The glacier had scraped it up as it advanced south, and as the ice melted some 18,000 years ago it left the soil in the valleys and on the gentle hills. In other places it left soil mixed with the stones and boulders that urban writers seem to find charming and romantic.

Connecticut agriculture has a long and honorable history. Early in the seventeenth century fertile soils drew colonists from Massachusetts. They settled in the Hartford area in 1633 and along the coast from Greenwich to Saybrook soon after. The population grew from 2,000 in 1640 to 24,000 in 1700. By 1713 two-thirds of the state was settled, by 1754 all of it was, and by 1800 we numbered 260,000 souls. Connecticut was the great source of provisions for the army of the revolution. In 1842 the potato crop gave the town of Greenwich the highest per capita income in the state.

At the end of the eighteenth century nine-tenths of the people earned their living from farms. Even those in other businesses or professions owned land that supplied part of their needs. Farming methods had changed little in two hundred years, and it was not until industrialization had pushed the population to a million, around 1890, and only three out of ten people were farming, that agriculture entered its modern phase. Those who grew grain crops and raised livestock moved west, where larger tracts of land were to be found. Smaller eastern farms were concentrating on dairy and poultry products, fresh fruits and vegetables, all high-income per acre crops.

Except in the warmest southern states, American farmers have always grown apples for their own needs, for cider, for livestock feed, and to store for winter use. In the late nineteenth century a commercial fruit industry developed to supply the growing cities. New England, with the right climate and access to markets, was ideal for growing apples and pears. Connecticut also grew large crops of peaches until new highways and refrigerated trucks moved peach farming further south, but tree-ripened peaches can still be found at Connecticut farm markets.

Apples and pears, which may be stored for long periods, are the chief fruits grown today, but pick-your-own harvesting has also made fragile strawberries, raspberries, and blueberries widely available. Because fruit farms maintain refrigerated storages, they have been successful with retail markets, and this has attracted young growers. Ever more complicated and expensive machinery is needed, however, to save labor in the orchard and the packing-house. This may produce higher quality fruit for the customer, but the cost of this equipment must be spread over larger acreages.

When I started farming, agricultural economists were saying that a twenty-acre orchard could provide a decent living for a farm family. This estimate went up steadily. Forty years later, when I had nearly a hundred acres of trees, I could see that the farm was too small; the really profitable fruit farms were much larger. By that time land prices had soared, and in any case there was no open land available nearby. All I could do was work the farm for all it could produce and promote the market for all we could sell there.

In Connecticut tobacco was long a major product; the state originated the practice of growing high-priced cigar wrapper and binder leaves in a microclimate maintained under cloth "tents" in partial shade. When the cigar market declined after World War II, much of the land was turned to nursery crops to supply suburban homes and landscaped business buildings, and this became our largest farm industry. The production per acre of most of our crops is above national averages, and our concentrated population gives us profitable markets.

A revolution in agriculture got under way in the 1930s, about when I started farming. Until then farmers' methods and personalities had not changed much since the nineteenth century; very little technical training or scientific information was needed to run a farm. Poor roads and long hours kept the farm family isolated from townspeople, but changes both on and off the farm were working to alter this. I have found that farmers, who live every day with forces beyond their control, are generally conditioned to accept change, technical and even social.

Early twentieth-century tractors, with cleated iron wheels, were only a more temperamental substitute for patient animals pulling old-style plows and harrows. By the late thirties an up-to-date tractor had rubber tires and a built-in hydraulic system to control farm tools which were mounted on the tractor itself. Research in plant and animal breeding and nutrition was beginning to improve the yields and the quality of farm products. During World War II there was a great surge in the production of chemicals of all kinds, providing new resources for the protection of farm crops from insects and diseases and competition from weeds.

All of this multiplied the efficiency of the individual farmer. Now, in the 1990s, only 2 percent of Americans are farmers, and they are able to feed all of us. An increasing part of the cost of food goes not to the farmer but to the processor and distributor, but we still have lower food bills than any other nation.

During the half century I spent in agriculture it followed most other American industries into an era of increasing mechanization, increasing specialization of product, increasing size of farms, and a decreasing need for labor. This has raised many economic and philosophic questions about the place of the family farm in society.

At a time when nine-tenths of Americans were farmers, Thomas Jefferson believed, as had ancient and medieval philosophers before him, that agriculture was the noblest occupation and that the future of democracy was bound up with the fate of the agricultural community. Many people today would like to think of the farmer as very much the same person Jefferson saw. Improved transportation and communication and access to public health, education, and recreation facilities have in fact erased most of the differences between rural and urban people.

I would be the last to deny the deep satisfactions of working with soil and plants, but I do not believe, as Jefferson did, that this made me a better citizen, a more staunch and upstanding democrat. I had found opportunities for public service in my small suburban town, I had found them earlier when I lived in a huge city, and I found them in the farming community.

Farmers have lost much of the independence about which politicians and writers are so lyrical, and they are far from self-sufficient. They now depend on others for processing and distributing their crops, leaving them with the single function of producing them. They buy not only machinery but farm supplies, seed, fertilizer, fuel, and even much of the food on their table.

The family farm provides an important part of our diet, and the rural town is a valuable part of our culture. It is a proper function of government to support agriculture, as it does other industries, by research, education, marketing assistance, and help in conserving resources. It has further been public policy to maintain the stability of the farm economy by protecting the farmer against loss when commodity prices fall and the consumer against higher costs when prices rise. It is a deception, however, to use public funds to provide consumers with cheap food if they are forced to pay to the tax collector, as their share of farm subsidies, what they save at the supermarket.

The myth of the family farmer as a unique independent individual persists. Farmers may work long hours and worry about weather and crop prices, but we remember mostly the amenities of their country environment and their historic niche in the community. We see urban workers enduring assembly-line pressures, un-healthy workplaces, crowded living quarters, and loss of pride in their work. If society feels a sense of guilt for tolerating such con-ditions, it can find comfort in thinking of the family farmer as spared from this fate. For this comfort we spend large sums of public money.

Farmers do not always appreciate pressures to keep them on the farm, the suggestion that it is somehow a shameful betrayal if they quit. They want to preserve the values they and their children find in country life, but they are not always cheerful about the work schedules and economic pressures with which they live. They do not want to be privileged members of society, but they do ask to share in rising standards of living.

The farmer who seeks to leave the farm no longer has to make the simple choice between the plow and the assembly line, as so many did in the rush to Detroit earlier in the century. There are more jobs now in construction, health, and service industries. Good transportation makes part-time farming a practical alterna-tive almost everywhere; hundreds of thousands of rural couples now hold urban jobs to supplement their farm incomes and still continue to enjoy the values of rural living.

I was able to expand the farm rapidly after my mar-riage to Martha in 1946. The big boom in Connecticut land prices did not start until the 1960s. Martha provided a rotating fund that I did not have to repay for many years. For only about $40,000 we were able to buy most of the three adjoining farms, keeping the good orchard land and selling a house and a dozen or so build-ing lots where the soil and drainage were not good. The last major purchase was in 1956 when I acquired the farm across the road from George Edmond's widow and sixteen landlocked acres acces-sible through the Edmond fields. That piece had been offered to me in 1950 when I advertised anonymously for land. The offer came from a Mrs. Boquist in Chicago who had inherited part of the old Merrill farm. She wrote that her land was very fertile and was near to the farm "where Mr. Josephy was making a great deal of money."

Three-quarters of the Edmond farm was very good land, the rest poorly drained and unsuitable for orchards. I planned to sell it for housing to help pay for the good acres. I sold the first lot to Roger

Merritt, a storekeeper, for $2,000 an acre, and the second one to a black friend, Alfred Slocum, an electrical engineer. When Merritt learned he was to have black neighbors he sold his lot, and I sold no more land for some years. By that time the prejudice had evaporated, and the lots were bringing much higher prices.

Around 1960 I was able to make a rent-free arrangement to use 15 acres of utility company land in return for keeping it free from brush. This brought the Blue Jay Orchards to a total of about 140 contiguous acres. Of course every one of those 140 acres could not be used for crops. Farm buildings and yards took some space, as did the roads needed for moving equipment and harvested fruit. As on nearly every New England farm, there were small areas too stony, too wet, or too steep to plant. I used every foot that I could by removing rocks or installing drainage tile and ditches. The original farms, like most others, were long and narrow with limited frontage on the highway, so Blue Jay ended up a mile long and a quarter mile wide, extending both north and south from Plumtrees Road.

In 1935 I joined the Connecticut Pomological Society, an old association part educational and part social. Pomology is the science of fruit culture. The community of fruit growers in Connecticut is not a large one, and my farm soon became known throughout the state; it was one of the few orchard enterprises to be started during the Great Depression. In 1957, only twenty-two years after I planted my first trees, I was elected to a term as president of the Society.

Also in 1957, I was appointed by Governor Abraham Ribicoff to be the fruit grower member of the State Board of Agriculture. This board was established by statute in 1866 to "advise the Agriculture Commissioner on policy." It included representatives of the major farm commodity groups—dairy, poultry, vegetable, nursery, fruit, and others—one of the many unpaid citizen boards that had long been a valuable feature of state government. It existed until 1979, and I was its last chairman.

The board was abolished as part of Governor Ella Grasso's effort to streamline state government. Grasso, our first woman governor, managed to acquire a public reputation as a compassionate person, but people who worked with her knew her as a tough and often ruthless politician. She wanted tight control of every agency; unpaid bipartisan boards like ours were not easily controlled. Fortunately, her successor, William O'Neill, appointed a new board with similar but even broader functions.

There were many other programs in which I took part and in which I often held office. One was the New York and New England Apple Institute, devoted to promotion and marketing. I also belonged to a variety of farm cooperatives, assisted the New York apple breeding program at Geneva by testing new apple varieties on my farm, and attended horticulture society meetings in several northeastern states.

I represented Fairfield County on the Farm Bureau state board for many years. The Farm Bureau is the largest and most conservative of American farm organizations. I disliked its political orientation and many of its national policies but supported it on most Connecticut farm issues. In particular, I was interested in helping cement Farm Bureau support for a farm-land preservation program. The Farm Bureau claims to represent all Connecticut agriculture, but in fact the majority of its members are dairy farmers and little effort is made to enroll members in the poultry and nursery industries, the other largest groups.

The need for agreement on congressional funding keeps most agricultural programs out of party politics. An exception is the Agriculture Stabilization and Conservation Service (ASCS). A branch of the U.S. Department of Agriculture, the ASCS helps farmers pay for improved conservation practices. Both ASCS paid officials and unpaid members of state committees change with control of the White House. I was appointed under the Carter administration on Senator Ribicoff's recommendation and replaced by a Republican four years later, though I can remember no decision we ever made that had any relation to a party program or policy.

As a farmer, I first became interested in the Connecticut Agricultural Experiment Station because of research done there on insects, plant diseases, plant growth, and nutrition. Founded in 1875, it was the first of what became a national system of state research institutions. The station's work is not limited to studying crop growth and protection; it extends to forests, soils, water, public health, and the environment. Its chemists analyze fertilizers, foods, drugs, and pesticides, much of this for other state agencies. Among the station's important discoveries have been Vitamin A and two other vitamins, a system for growing superior tobacco in partial shade, and a practical method of hybridizing corn. This last invention resulted in tremendous increases in the world's corn crops. In recent years it has pioneered in the identification and study of the ticks that carry the pathogen which causes Lyme disease.

The station is governed by a board of control, which includes representatives of Yale, Wesleyan, and Connecticut universities and several appointees of the governor. I joined that board in 1962 and have had the privilege of working with three station directors. I found that as a farmer and a layman I could add another viewpoint to the thinking of the scientists and perhaps bring the Board of Control closer to the organization. I have learned a lot from station staff people, and I have also had the pleasure of designing the station's many publications.

The station is a state agency. Most of its budget comes from Hartford, a little from Washington. It also has several endowments managed by the Board of Control, which enables it to underwrite activities and make improvements not covered by public funds. I have seen it make good use of the income from these endowments, and my will provides for another one. I would like to leave to public use a major part of the money the state paid me in 1983 for the preservation of my land.

Paul Waggoner, who was station director from 1972 to 1987, became one of my closest friends. When he became director I was vice president of the board (the governor is always the president). I worked with him on station problems, and we took part in many other farm and environmental projects. We share an attitude and a sense of the possible that makes us natural collaborators.

Paul is both a plant pathologist and a climatologist. His idea of retirement is to work harder than ever. He lectures around the world and is a leader in the studies of climate change which now concerns politicians as well as scientists. His broad interests have enabled him to make a substantial impact on current scientific thought.

13 🍎 *Trees, Crops, and Customers*

What Eve ate in the garden was probably not the apple we know, but it became the enduring symbol of human fallibility. To us the apple is not only prominent in our literature; in the spring it is a delight in our landscape, and year-round it is a staple in our diet, which makes it a major item in our farm economy. The tree has a long life, it responds readily to pruning and training, and from free verse to still life it is celebrated by all the arts.

America grows more oranges than apples, but oranges are raised in only a few states; apples are grown commercially in thirty-six. As on most northern fruit farms, they were my chief crop. I also grew pears, peaches, a few plums, strawberries, and raspberries, but this chapter will be mostly about apples, the major part of my business. Growing and selling them occupied most of my year and produced most of the discussion at growers' meetings and most of the research by horticultural scientists.

When planning a new orchard I first had to decide what varieties to plant. During the long history of apple growing there have been thousands of varieties, sometimes called cultivars. Henry Thoreau reported seeing 1,400 growing in the gardens of the London Horticultural Society in 1836. Trees differ in hardiness, branch structure, and earliness and regularity of bearing.

Only a few dozen varieties are important commercially. The self-service supermarket has encouraged the production of high-colored eye-catching fruit; many less flashy but higher quality apples are grown in backyard gardens or are available to knowledgeable people at farm markets. Each orchard that I planted had to include varieties wanted by wholesale customers and some for sale only at our own market. Some were apples that mature by the end of July, to supply apple lovers who can hardly wait for the new crop.

These early apples do not keep well, so we grew a succession of varieties ripening weekly. By mid-September, McIntosh time, the appetite for apples peaks, and we must have nine-tenths of the crop ready to pick during a seven-week period ending in late October, before freezing nights would damage fruit left on trees. With a succession of apples, including a number of new ones we were testing in cooperation with the New York fruit-breeding program, we grew about forty varieties.

The most popular of these were McIntosh, Cortland, Macoun, Red Delicious, and Ida-red. We also grew Milton, Paula-red, and R.I. Greening for wholesale customers and for our retail market Baldwin, Mutsu, Roxbury Russett, and Melrose. Most of these make good cider; we learned to combine sweet and tart apples to maintain uniform flavor all season. A substantial part of the national crop is processed for sauce, juice, or pie fillings, but most New England apples are sold to consumers as fresh fruit.

After choosing varieties I had to decide what size trees I wanted. A few growers propagate trees for themselves; the general custom is to buy one- or two-year-old stock from a commercial nursery. Until the sixties the practice was to grow small trees from apple seeds and graft buds on these seedlings at ground level. The resulting shoots would then be trained to make trees. Grafting was necessary because only the bud, not the seed, carries the genes of the apple variety. These "standard" trees do not bear much fruit until about their tenth year. Grant Hitchings, an elderly grower in western New York, used to say, "Old men plant apples 'cause young men can't wait." I planted seedling-rooted trees until 1956. By then I was fifty-three, and, in spite of Mr. Hitchings's optimism, I thought I was too old to wait for new trees to bear. I did not have his kind of patience.

Researchers in England meanwhile had identified and classified rootstocks which produce trees that are smaller and start to bear in their third or fourth year. They provide trees one-fourth to three-fourths the size of "standards," some of them adapted to particular varieties and soils. These trees are not propagated sexually from seeds but clonally by grafting buds directly onto shoots growing from selected roots. I tried a few of these dwarf trees, then planted 400 in 1970. They did well, and I planted more every year starting in 1976, most of them to replace old trees on seedling roots. I continued this annual replanting program until I sold the farm in 1985.

The old seedling-rooted trees were expected to spread to forty feet at maturity, which allows only 27 trees per acre. Trees on dwarfing roots can be planted 180 or 240 to the acre; still smaller ones (which require trellises or stakes for support) at even higher densities. We hand dug the holes for my first trees in 1935; later we used a tractor-mounted soil auger which drills holes twenty-four inches in diameter. Still later we had a planting machine that is drawn slowly down the row and sets the trees in a deep furrow.

Apple trees well cared for have a long life; I have had many that were producing good fruit at fifty years. That does not mean, however, that they remain profitable. As they get older they need severe pruning to keep them from crowding and shading one another, to let light into the tree, and to let spray reach all the branches. This gradually reduces their production. The smaller trees, which most growers now plant, permit more light to reach the fruit and foliage and are easier to prune, spray, and pick.

Training young trees by pruning, and sometimes by spreading branches to strengthen crotch angles, is for me the most interesting orchard job. One can watch them grow and change form as time and the weight of crops alter their structure, and one learns to anticipate these changes. Living with trees as they grow, sometimes for fifty years, and helping to shape that growth are experiences offered by no other kind of farming. Fruit trees of any kind should be pruned every year to encourage the strongest-bearing branches, to control height, and to let light into the tree. Photosynthesis, the basic process of converting carbon dioxide and water into leaves and wood and fruit, can only take place where there is light.

A spring job that I especially enjoyed was grafting. This is an ancient technique easily learned from horticulture handbooks. The trick is to unite the cambium of a twig with several buds, called a scion, with the cambium of a tree branch or trunk. The cambium is the thin layer of green live tissue between bark and wood. Damage by mice or machinery is often repaired by grafting across injured areas. Grafting branches of apple or pear trees with scions carrying buds of another variety, a procedure called top-working, is a time-saving method of obtaining more marketable fruit or testing newly bred kinds. I became expert at this and changed the crops of hundreds of trees.

Another major concern in the spring is pollination. To produce fruit most trees need to receive pollen from another variety while in bloom. Honey bees are the most efficient collectors and distributors of pollen. Growers rent colonies of bees for a week or two at blossom time, but if the weather is cold or wet or windy, the bees will stay in the hives and do no work, and the trees will set no fruit.

In addition to good soil and good drainage an orchard must have some elevation, with a lower area nearby down to which cold air can sink when frosts and freezes come. Frost can kill blossoms and tiny developing fruits; various kinds of heaters are often used. One year we had what is called an inversion. There was a layer of air near the ground cold enough to kill apple blossoms, with a layer at least ten degrees warmer only twenty-five feet above it. I hired a helicopter to fly back and forth mixing the two layers. It saved my crop.

The pilot was a former navy flier who had done this work many times in New York orchards. He started his flight at about two o'clock, when the temperature at ground level was down to 35 degrees, and flew until after sunrise. A few neighbors were alarmed by the noise. One of them, whose son had recently entertained himself by setting fire to some mulch hay in one of the orchards, wrote to the local newspaper complaining about his lost sleep.

Proper nutrition of plants is essential for growth. Manures and the traditional fish in the cornhill are ancient sources of plant food. Today, prepared fertilizers combining needed quantities of the basic ingredients of nitrogen, phosphorus, and potash with small amounts of other elements, are generally used. The correct formula is determined by analyzing soil and, in the case of trees, by analyzing leaves. Most New England soils are more acidic than desirable, and lime is added to neutralize the acid to a pH of about 6.5.

Orchards have not generally needed irrigation in Connecticut, where we usually have adequate rainfall. Peach trees, big water users, are an exception. During the droughts of the early sixties I bought a large pump and a mile or so of aluminum pipe to deliver water from farm ponds to the peaches and some of the apples. Dwarf trees, which do not have deep roots, may show a need for water. Trickle irrigation, bringing water directly to tree roots through small tubes, is often used now.

Spraying is essential to protect fruit and foliage. The need for this has increased as the concentration of trees in large commercial orchards has made them prime targets for pest invasions. Modern fruit breeding has produced varieties with superior flavor and texture but with thinner skins more easily damaged. At the same time, the urbanization of the population has led consumers, unacquainted with farmers' practices and problems, to demand perfect, unblemished fruits and vegetables. Fortunately, all the insects and diseases that damage crops are not present and active throughout the growing season. Their life cycles vary, and weather conditions affect them. Some pests, however, develop resistance to certain chemicals. As a careful farmer I was constantly checking to see when to spray, what chemicals to use, and how to avoid unnecessary spraying.

The development of agricultural chemicals was stimulated during World War II by the need to protect the health of troops in tropical countries. We now have newer formulas, effective for the control of specific pests but less toxic to humans and less damaging to the environment. I will discuss this further in the next chapter.

Normal bloom frequently results in more apples than can reach desirable size. Thinning them, removing many tiny fruits early in the season so that those remaining have enough space and nutrients, is an old practice. Historically, large crews of schoolboys have been employed in late June and July to pick off the surplus. In recent years chemicals have been invented which inhibit cell development and eliminate the smallest and weakest fruits. This has not only helped produce apples and pears of marketable size but has stimulated regular annual bearing on those varieties with a tendency to bear biennially.

Young succulent spring shoots on apple trees are a favorite food of the white-tailed deer, and in the fall the bucks rub the bark off young trees with their antlers. In the thirties a herd of eight lived in the woods behind my orchards. A dozen small trees, each with only a few branches, can barely make a meal for a hungry deer, and I came to feel they were my worst enemies. I shot a number of them at night and reported this to the game warden, who approved when he saw the damage. Everett Havens dressed them for me, and we divided the venison.

After a few years new neighbors, many of them with dogs, built houses in the woodlands and the deer disappeared, but in the seventies they came back. Animal lovers' campaigns against hunting had increased the deer population far beyond the capacity of the countryside to sustain it. Hungry deer learned to live in small patches of trees and brush and to eat farm and garden crops and ornamental shrubs.

I learned from research done in New York that the odor of human hair would repel deer. We collected hair from barbers, preferably hair not too well washed, and filled hundreds of small mesh bags, one for each tree. That kept most of them away. Later soap was also found to repel deer, and we used that also.

Two species of mice (sometimes called voles) damage fruit trees and many other plants. In orchards we have meadow mice who live in the grass and pine mice whose burrows go as deep as two feet. Both of them girdle trunks and roots, eating cambium when other food is scarce. They multiply so fast that controlling them with repellents and poisons is an all-year job. We win a few battles, but we never win the war.

Trying to control two-legged animals is more difficult and much more discouraging. Vandalism, which seems to baffle sociologists, is suffered by farmers along with the rest of society. We have had small trees broken or pulled out of the ground and frequent damage to equipment. Smashing mailboxes is a popular sport. I once asked a boy why he attacked mine. "I had a fight with my girlfriend," he explained.

Pumpkins are also a favorite target. One time the police caught half a dozen high school boys smashing my Halloween pumpkins. In the town court I offered to withdraw charges if the boys would work for me to pay for the damage. All but one of their fathers chose to pay me in cash to protect the boys from such cruel punishment. This hardly discouraged them from further lawbreaking. I distributed a letter to a hundred neighbors asking for help. This may have done some good, but of course it did not remove the tensions that inspire such antisocial conduct.

Getting the crop picked is every grower's biggest problem. The challenge is to find enough pickers and to get the fruit picked with a minimum of bruising and dropping. At first we had help from neighbors, then other local people. In the 1950s, when we began producing substantial quantities of apples, we brought in men each day from a labor camp owned by a large nursery in the nearby town of Ridgefield.

These men were recruited by an employment agency on the Bowery in New York City. They were almost all alcoholics, part of a large underclass of drifters who returned to the Bowery between jobs. They came from all kinds of backgrounds; a few had good educations, and most had steady jobs until family disruptions, petty offenses against society, or just simply thirst brought them to their low status. A few could stay sober through the harvest season, most for only two or three weeks, some for only a few days. There was a constant turnover in the crew and a fresh supply of men arriving at the camp.

Some of these men had picked apples for years and were skillful. The majority were uncoordinated and handled the fruit roughly, and many had to be sent to digging holes for the Ridgefield nursery. They were mostly decent and amiable, reconciled to their lives with no antisocial attitudes, and usually honest. Some I got to know well, and if they borrowed small sums from me between seasons they usually paid their debts.

The itinerant farm workers of the South and Far West avoided the shorter harvest season of the Northeast, and the Bowery-based pool of men was long the main source of seasonal labor for Eastern farms and summer resorts. Many of the men would reappear every fall until their health broke down and they dropped out of the ranks of the partly employed.

In 1961 the labor camp ceased to exist. We needed fifteen to twenty men, and for years I had to go to certain bars on the Bowery favored by apple pickers, hunt for men I knew and recruit others, and bring them to a series of improvised camps we set up in empty houses near the farm. We had beds and bedding and kitchenware; strategies for providing meals stretched our ingenuity and my wife's strength and patience.

A few years later the state mental hospital in nearby Newtown began to allow some patients to work outside the institution, and they picked part of our crop. Their skill and adaptability varied enormously, but some of them managed to do quite well. At worst they were sober, and we did not have to worry about their housing and food.

In the sixties the postwar boom in manufacturing had still left millions of workers with limited education and skills looking for work. Farm workers in the South, replaced by new sophisticated machinery, were also adrift, leaving a huge pool of potential apple pickers. We found, however, that few of those available in New England had grown up with the skills and adaptability of country people, and most could not learn to pick apples. Many of them were scornful of working without machinery, or of working without wheels under them, or of working with their feet on the ground or on ladders. A few were even afraid to climb. One man came to work at 8:00, looked at his tree until 8:30, then quit and asked to be paid for the half hour. He held the record.

This was an early sign of the loss of worker adaptability that was to handicap American industry a generation later. The government pressed us to employ these people, and we made strenuous efforts to do so, but we had little success. Most of the applicants were referred to us because they had filed for unemployment compensation. They were expected to appear for interviews, but they could not be compelled to come or to work if they were hired. I believed in unemployment insurance as a device for protecting workers from fluctuations in the economy beyond their control, but I could see that it would not always get people to give up its benefits and try new jobs.

By the seventies there was a program for importing men from Jamaica for the harvest season. With some difficulty we growers convinced Washington officials that unemployed Americans could not and would not pick apples, that without the foreign pickers the farm economy would suffer huge losses and the food supply would be diminished. The Jamaicans were carefully screened at home by a government agency. They were strong, agile, and dexterous and quickly learned the tricks of apple picking. They were also agreeable, sober, and highly motivated to earn money. Six or eight of them could out-pick twenty Bowery men. Paid by the bushel, many of them made more in a few weeks than they could earn in a year in Jamaica. We provided their living quarters, they cooked for themselves. It was a happy ending to many years of harvest-time turmoil and uncertainty.

When I got my first crop I was not much interested in marketing it. I wished that I could sell all my apples to a dealer as soon as they were picked, as some growers did. I soon learned that the way to pay my bills was to sell direct to consumers. Apples and pears that mature after the middle of September can be stored for long periods if picked at the right time and refrigerated promptly. This permits orderly marketing of the crop. By the mid-forties I was storing fruit in a New Milford ice plant and keeping some in an air-cooled room I had improvised in the barn basement. It was there that we began selling to retail customers.

By 1950 we had outgrown those facilities, and I mortgaged the farmland to pay for a new building. An architect friend made me some sketches, but his plan looked more like a factory than a farm building, so I designed the structure myself. It had refrigerated space for 9,000 bushels of apples, a large room for sorting, packing, and retail sales, and a truck garage. We opened it for business in the fall of 1951. Three years later we added space for a cider mill, then a second 9,000-bushel storage room, and still later we attached another garage. Finally in 1979 we built two controlled atmosphere storage rooms.

Controlled atmosphere (CA) storage was first used in the fifties. Pomologists had always known that respiration continues after fruit is picked. Oxidation taking place in the cells changes their structure, advances ripening, and eventually results in decay. Reducing the oxygen available slows this process. CA rooms are made airtight, and oxygen is reduced from the normal level of about 20 percent to about 3 percent. Surplus carbon dioxide, the product of the oxidation, is removed mechanically.

CA storage adds three to six months to the storage life of apples, depending on the variety. It permits selling a crop over a longer period and provides consumers with apples in good condition year-round. One year we had a leak of the ammonia refrigerant, and before it was detected a roomful of apples—some 7,000 bushels—was ruined. Except for that rare accident, CA storage worked well and kept some of our apples until summer.

I found that many people would come to the farm to buy fresh fruit, cider, and other farm products. A few farmers, notably growers of fruit, had successful retail markets in urbanized areas like ours where there were lots of customers. With facilities for keeping fruit in good condition and an attractive market building, we were ready to promote retail sales. I learned how to make excellent cider, using a modern sanitary mill, firm cold apples, and no preservatives. Eventually we were selling over 25,000 gallons a year, most of it in the fall, but we continued pressing fresh cider until late spring, as long as we had apples, and froze some for summer sale.

Cider making is an exact science. The rules are simple, but they must be followed rigorously. On one occasion, to save a little time, we pressed a batch of apples that had not been properly cooled. The flavor of the cider was not up to our standards, and we never took that shortcut again.

Diversification was the buzzword for farmers with retail markets. We tried to grow everything our customers would buy, limited only by the availability of land and suitable soil. Sales of sweet corn were enormous during the short corn season, but all our good land was in orchards. We were supplied for years by a Woodbridge man who went to farms in the Connecticut valley every morning, loaded our order picked before daylight, and had it in our cooler by nine o'clock.

Fresh eggs were hard to find in Fairfield County. I built a new henhouse for 1,100 birds and later another; eventually we were selling over 30,000 dozen eggs a year, and the eggs attracted steady, year-round customers to the market. Chickens are not lovable creatures, and in fifty years I only found one man who liked dealing with them, but they were an important part of our business. Our birds were kept indoors, but not in wire cages as they are in large, automated egg factories.

In addition to tree fruits, we grew strawberries, raspberries, Christmas trees, and some vegetables, all for retail sale. When we first opened the storage building our young trees were not producing enough apples to fill it, so I rented and operated four small orchards in nearby towns until our crops at Blue Jay were adequate.

The farm market was a great challenge, and it soon took a large part of my thought and energy. I built all the shelves and stands, lettered the signs, selected paint colors, and wrote and designed the advertising. I tried to establish the atmosphere of a modern but informal rural market, not at all quaint but different from town

food-stores. I enjoyed the chance to express my personal taste, and I found the customers responded.

At first we advertised the market with small classified ads; when I tried tripling the budget there was a jump in sales, which surprised me. From then on I increased our use of newspapers and the radio as our sales grew. My experience in the design of printing helped to make our small newspaper ads conspicuous and readable. A series of short essays about what we do on the farm brought us a lot of attention. Here is a facsimile of one and copies of the text of some others.

IN LIKE A LION...

Days are longer and the sun warmer, and if that snow will go we'll get some pruning done. Meanwhile our new chicks are here. Raised indoors, they will be fed, warmed, medicated, vaccinated, debeaked, and pampered. They'll start to lay in August, move to an insulated house in December, and last year's hens will go. Most of our eggs are sold at the farm the day they are laid. Some apples taste better after months in storage, but Time is the enemy of the egg.

STRAIGHT APPLE AD

This is a straight ad for apples, not one of those essays. The other day a man said "I love to read your ads but I never buy apples." Maybe we need a more hard-sell approach such as "How about it, Friend, if you love to read our ads why don't you get the message? Do yourself a favor and try a few apples instead of all that high calorie stuff, and some fresh cider instead of that you-know-what. We have great crisp-aire apples; they taste like fresh-picked fruit in October." . . . How does that sound?

WHO PICKS APPLES?

The farm is really humming now. Five of us can grow the crop, but it takes 25 or 30 to harvest it. Picking apples takes special skills, as many factory workers have found out. Most of our men are old timers. Unlike West Coast migrants who follow the crops with families, they are usually unattached, some devoted to the bottle, some just to freedom from responsibility. They get seasonal jobs of all kinds in many places, turn up here in September. Don't know what we'd do without them!

When I bought it, the farm had a typical old farm orchard of about thirty apple trees. In 1935 I sold some fruit from those trees to a roadside stand for seventy cents a bushel, my first wholesale transaction. For the next fifty years I did business with stores of all sizes and with big supermarket chains. For some years nine of us growers had a marketing cooperative called the Laurel State Association. We had all been selling apples to First National supermarkets, delivered direct to the stores. We arranged to deal with them as a group, with uniform packages and prices. This was successful until new managers decided to have all apples handled by their central warehouse, a practice usually followed by other chains. We regretted this because delivery from the farm direct to the store reduced handling costs and got our fruit to consumers in the best condition possible.

Occasionally we had a surplus of some variety that had to be sold abroad. An apple broker in New York would get us the order. Once sorted and packed, the fruit had to be examined at the farm by a federal inspector, a procedure that made us nervous because the apples might no longer be in prime condition. We would then have to truck them to a Brooklyn or New Jersey pier, hoping that the inevitable freezing weather would do no damage. We tried to avoid selling apples that way.

Sales at our retail market soon exceeded our wholesale totals, and I only sold wholesale what I could not sell retail. Thus, although my crops increased to 30,000 and 35,000 bushels, my wholesale income stayed at an average of about $50,000. Retail sales, on the other hand, rose from $10,000 in 1951, the year after we built the new market, to $40,000 ten years later. By 1969 retail sales were over $100,000, by 1980 over $200,000, and in 1984, the last full year I owned the farm, over $300,000.

This was a very satisfying accomplishment. It would have been more satisfying if inflation had not raised my expenses as fast as my income, so that some years my tax returns showed a net loss. I was permitted to deduct the cost of farm improvements. This reduced my income taxes, but eventually the improvements were taxed as capital gains.

The success of the farm enterprise, I always believed, was largely due to my decision in 1934 to locate in a town like Bethel. Even after Blue Jay had become the last farm in the town and Bethel had become a lawn-to-lawn suburb, the place remained part of the local economy and local culture. People liked the idea of having a farm nearby, and they liked being able to buy farm-grown produce. We also had an increasing number of foreign-born residents who were among our most enthusiastic customers.

My biggest farm expense by far was for labor. I had no full-time help until 1946, but I did need some part-time help from neighbors. Farm workers were traditionally paid less than those in any other industry. In 1935 I paid two schoolboys twenty cents and thirty cents an hour for helping plant my first orchard. At that time my neighbor Havens was paying his experienced hired man thirty cents; he was furious when the government paid fifty cents for make-work jobs to put some cash into the pockets of the unemployed. That, of course, was during the Great Depression. As the Connecticut economy recovered, the rapid growth of industry needed workers, and farm wages approached those in manufacturing.

The fruit grower is not tied to the seven-day routine of the dairy farmer. Caring for our small flock of two thousand hens was our only regular chore; otherwise, our work varied from day to day. We sprayed all the trees twelve to fourteen times between April and September, mostly at night and early morning when there is less wind and no sun to evaporate the spray before it hits the trees.

The orchards had strips of sod between rows; we mowed those several times, starting in late May. Pruning was chiefly done in winter and early spring, when lack of foliage made it easier to see tree structure. This was the job that required the most skill and experience; it was done with hand shears and with powerful pneumatic cutters. Young dwarf trees also benefited from a second pruning in late summer. Removing pruning brush was a major problem.

Berries and vegetables had to be planted, cultivated, and harvested, and the poultry cared for. Maintenance of buildings and equipment was done between other more urgent jobs. Until the last of the crop was sold in late spring, fruit had to be sorted and packed both for our market and for wholesale customers. Even when we reached maximum production I did not need many people to maintain the orchards or to grow the crops, except of course at picking time. The orchard crew grew from one to half a dozen. They came from many states, and all of them had some previous farm experience. There was a constant turnover, but one man stayed with me for twenty-three years, and we parted only because he could not or would not control his extreme obesity.

The sorting-packing room and the market needed a bigger crew. Our work hours, from 8 A.M. to 5:30 P.M., were set by the retail market and in the fall for the comfort of the pickers, who did not like wet, cold trees in the early morning. These hours and the variety of tasks made Blue Jay a pleasant place to work.

During forty years, starting with my first full-time hired man in 1946, I had hundreds of men and women, boys and girls, helping me. Many of these were part-time students, adult moonlighters, or summer vacation workers. Most of those in the market and packing room were girls and women, but in the eighties a change in the notions of what was suitable work brought a number of women outdoors to drive trucks and tractors and do other "man's work."

Apples are a highly perishable commodity; they lose crispness and flavor soon after they come out of refrigerated storage. It was seldom practical to sort and pack on a regular schedule in anticipation of need. Apple sales, whether in supermarkets or in farm markets like ours, depend on weather, advertising, and the competition of other fruits. When we had to pack a large order for a chain store warehouse, it was usually on short notice and we had to do evening work.

The heavy traffic at our own market was on weekends, and that rose and fell with the weather and the season. On busy days we had to pack apples, press and jug cider continuously. It was never possible to predict which apple varieties and which packages people would buy. October was our busiest time, but the other fall months were only a little less strenuous. After Christmas things slowed down, but we had substantial sales all through the winter and spring.

In the eighties we extended our fall pick-your-own program. Our customers had been picking strawberries in June and raspberries in July and September; we decided with some trepidation to let them pick apples and pears. The crowds who came were hard to manage, but they picked a lot of fruit with very little tree damage, and I regretted not starting the program years earlier.

We had a grading machine to sort and size apples before we packaged them. They passed over rollers which rotated them so that an inspector could cull fruit, the second grade to be sold at lower prices, the third grade used for cider. The perfect apples were then separated into the sizes required for the various packages, and some were fed into a machine that filled and weighed plastic bags holding three or four pounds.

All this required the close coordination of half a dozen or more people. Working together at their stations around the grader, often under pressure, friction would develop, and there would be an occasional explosion. Part of my job was to maintain a friendly, cooperative atmosphere, but now and then there were personalities I could not handle. The very fact of being employed, of having to cede to an employer a substantial amount of control over one's life, is not easy for everyone to bear. Sometimes a person would express dissatisfaction with his or her pay, sometimes with the pay of a coworker who seemed to be getting preferential treatment.

It would take a whole book to describe individually all the people who worked for me and to acknowledge my debt to each of them. My trade union days impressed upon me the truth that the economic interests of employer and employee were not identical. I could never forget that I was extracting what Marx called surplus value from the people I employed. On the other hand, I had to keep the farm solvent and preserve their jobs. I am not sure how well this conflict was understood by the people who worked for me, but I did know that I had a reputation for being a "good" boss, whatever that meant. How much my social principles affected the farm income I can only guess.

14 🍎 *Protecting Land and People*

My first concern for the preservation of natural resources grew out of my day-to-day experiences as a farmer and not from any theories about the needs of humanity. I learned that the supply of soil and water is limited and not easily renewed and that nutrients taken from the soil by crops must be replaced. Soil and water not only produce the food and fiber that we consume, they also maintain all other plant and animal life, provide industrial materials and power, keep the air fit to breathe and the water fit to drink, and nourish the parks and wilderness which in turn nourish our bodies and spirits.

People from the Agricultural Extension Service and from the state university talked about conserving resources while they were teaching me how to grow fruit. The U.S. Soil Conservation Service (SCS) was showing farmers how to reduce soil erosion and protect streams. The SCS had been established in the thirties by Franklin Roosevelt and Secretary of Agriculture Henry Wallace and was the first effective conservation program since the days of Theodore Roosevelt and Gifford Pinchot before the First World War.

In the mid-forties the SCS designed a farm plan for me, mapping my soils and recommending a program for increasing efficiency and productivity. This included drainage and soil improvement, reducing soil erosion, digging three ponds, and clearing and grading pieces of stony or swampy land that had once been used for pasture. This was my introduction to what became known as the environment movement. I was enthusiastic about the SCS, and for many years I was a member of a county board of farmers who worked with the government technicians assigned to help us carry out conservation practices. This was my first serious participation in any broad program for improving farming methods, an ideal introduction to practices which were not only important for the preservation of the earth but also offered economic returns to farmers by keeping their land productive.

Many farmers acted as if their topsoil was unlimited; when it gave out in the past they could move to new territories. On sloping land they turned their furrows downhill because it was easier for their horses and oxen. On my farm, like many others, the topsoil was deep along stone walls at the bottom of slopes. They largely ignored the transport of soil by wind and water, and they gave little thought to stabilizing soil with organic mulches, as occurs naturally in forests. To reduce the competition between weeds and crop plants they eliminated the weeds and left the bare soil vulnerable to erosion.

Agriculture, which came late in human history, is one of our greatest cultural achievements. Farms and gardens, parks and landscapes, plant and animal breeding are changes in nature that few would want to see reversed. With them has come depletion of natural resources such as the erosion of topsoil, abuses which we are now trying to reverse. Respect for nature does not mean leaving it to change "naturally"; one might as well say that children should be left to grow without help or guidance.

Lovers of nature, as they perceive it, do not always admire the changes in land-use that farmers make to increase efficiency and productivity. There is some conflict between those who love other people's stone walls and those who have to cultivate small fields and cut brush, between those who cherish every bit of swamp and woods and the farmer's sense of order and the thrifty use of the land. There is even some confusion as to what is really natural. Stone walls were not formed by nature but by the farmer's need to clear fields and build fences. Most of our woodland is not virgin forest but followed the abandoning of infertile areas that had once been cultivated or pastured. Swamps often owe their origin to our damming or diversion of streams.

A farm is a landscape; the arrangement of fields and roads and buildings is an exercise in design. Orchards and vineyards, where rows of trees and vines predominate and are fixed for generations, are among our great artistic creations. On our farm we aimed to run tree rows north and south to catch the most hours of sunlight and to orient them to the terrain of the drumlin. This helped avoid water runoff and eased the passage of equipment. The orderly arrangement of elements, as in any design, brought aesthetic pleasure as well as efficiency.

Connecticut industry was born early in the eighteenth century with substantial mineral resources and plenty of water-power. During the nineteenth century it grew steadily, and in the twentieth century it supplied munitions for two world wars. By the end of World War II the effects of this industrialization, and the population growth it brought, were impacting the rural areas of the state, converting farmland to other uses and polluting air and water. These threats to the quality of life were bringing thoughtful people together for discussion and action.

In 1949 Martha and I went to the first meeting, in Hartford, of the Connecticut Natural Resources Council. Going east the sixty-five miles from Bethel to Hartford was a journey. There were no major east-west highways crossing the pattern set by the state's north-south development along its rivers. The population backbone was defined by the New Haven Railroad's Legislator Special. When the assembly was in session this train left Greenwich in the early morning, followed the shore towns east to New Haven, then headed north through Wallingford and Meriden to Hartford. Another "special" met it there carrying people from the upper Connecticut valley.

In the seventies a section of the interstate road system was completed from Danbury through Hartford and on toward Boston. This was a boon for me, as I had long been making frequent trips to farm meetings centered around the capital.

In 1949, however, we had to go to the Hartford meeting by the long route. The speakers there were the academics we expected to find but also people with major responsibilities in manufacturing, banking, and the huge insurance industry. What impressed us most were their arguments that Connecticut must have open space and recreation facilities to attract competent employees and to ensure them a good life. This kind of self-interest has given strength to the environment program ever since.

The Natural Resources Council continued its educational work under the leadership of Alice McCallister. In 1974 over seven hundred people came to a council meeting in Northford, where I contributed, as usual, a talk on farm preservation. Conservation had become a major issue in Connecticut. There were at the time a few regional groups like the Housatonic Valley Association working to protect rivers, lakes, and forests, but the council was the first to address the problems of the state as a whole.

In 1970 James Horsfall, director of the Connecticut Agricultural Experiment Station, initiated the formation of Governor John Dempsey's Committee on Environmental Policy. There were 150 members, people from every field of public or private activity that could in any way touch the environment, and I was one of them.

The final report of the committee recommended detailed actions affecting population, health, education, transportation, pollution, land-use, parks, planning, and development. Many of that committee's recommendations have been enacted into law; others have been pressed by private citizens' organizations. I was instrumental in strengthening the recommendation on farmland preservation. This was my first opportunity to speak up for the need to save farms, a cause for which I fought for many years.

One outgrowth of the committee's work was sentiment in the legislature for a state department concerned with environmental matters. Tom Meskill, who had become governor, opposed this until persuaded by his friend and backer Dan Lufkin. The Department of Environmental Protection was then established and funded; Lufkin became its first commissioner. He was energetic, imaginative, and inclined toward grandiose plans. He was not a man to stay long in any one place, and he was soon succeeded by Douglas Costle, who served until 1976 when he became administrator of the federal Environmental Protection Agency under President Carter.

The most critical factor affecting farming in Connecticut, indeed in most of the Northeast, is the increased cost and decreased availability of land. The needs of the growing population for space for housing, industry, and commerce, which drove grain and livestock farmers to the West in the nineteenth century, are never satisfied. There were a million people in Connecticut a century ago; there are over three million now. The permanent existence of farms had always been taken for granted, but between 1935, when I started farming, and 1970 half of the state's farmland was converted to other uses.

In the twentieth century, Connecticut cannot meet all of its food needs, but what it does produce prevents complete dependence on distant states and provides fresh crops of locally grown fruits and vegetables. The shortage of land became a personal problem for me when I wanted to expand the farm. I was able to acquire adjoining farms between 1947 and 1956, but later I found there was no more land nearby and very little anywhere in the state.

After the report of the Dempsey-Horsfall committee, a small group of my friends, farmers, agricultural officials, and scientists met to discuss what might be done about the loss of farms and farmers. There were signs that public concern was spreading and that finally the press was beginning to pay attention. The Ribicoff administration had established in the fifties a system of taxing farms, forests, and open spaces at use value rather than development value. By 1988 a third of the land in the state was receiving this tax break. This gave some economic relief to farmers, but it did not effectively slow the sales of farms.

In August of 1973, at the summer field day of the Experiment Station, I gave the annual Johnson Lecture before an audience of a thousand or so friends of agriculture. I made a strong plea for a program to preserve farmland, ending with these words: "If we do not move soon, and quickly, we may find in the twenty-first century that we have only a few farms left. Then we will hurry to make them into museum farms, like Old Sturbridge Village, preserved to try to show our grandchildren what Connecticut used to be like. Farms then will no longer be a real part of the environment, and of course we will lose the important contribution they make to our food supply.

"We have a unique state. It is more crowded than most, richer than most, more urbanized than most, and yet wilder than most. The quick alternation of town, farm, forest, and water is a pleasure and a stimulation to all of us. . . . Protecting the environment has now become urgent public business. We are spending money to do it, and we will continue to do so. If we want productive, well-kept farms to be part of this environment, these farms must be on a sound economic base. Growth and change beyond the control of the farmer have eroded that base in the twentieth century. Farming in Connecticut in the twenty-first century will depend on rebuilding that base now, before it is too late."

It turned out that my speech came at a most opportune time. The press gave it wide coverage, and the text was circulated at conservation meetings. It seemed to our little group that the time had come for action. In November we asked Governor Tom Meskill to set up a commission to make a study and some proposals. In April of 1974 he finally appointed a twenty-five-man (there were no women!) task force for the preservation of agricultural land. He replaced a few of the people we suggested with his political friends, but there were many able members. The chairman was Charles Stroh, an influential lawyer and farmer who had often gone to bat for agriculture. Don Tuttle, a radio broadcaster whose voice was heard in farm barns at milking time for many years, joined us. He proved to be an ideal organizer and spokesman for the project. He and I developed an instant friendship which lasted until his death in 1988.

Working with a sense of urgency, our task force finished its work by the end of 1974. Our chief recommendation was to counter the purchase of farmland by developers with a program for state purchase of farmers' development rights. That meant that the state would pay the owner of productive land the difference between its value for agriculture and what a real-estate investor would pay. The farmer would continue to own the land, subject only to a restriction against building on it anything other than a farm building. We proposed financing the program by a 1 percent tax on all real estate transfers.

Our proposals received a great deal of publicity, and some of us talked about them at meetings around the state to develop support. In 1976 the legislature directed the Board of Agriculture to inventory the cropland suitable for preservation and to estimate the cost of purchasing development rights. Finally in 1978 the first legislation was passed, appropriating $5 million to be obtained not by the transfer tax we recommended but by direct bonding of the amount authorized each year. The responsibility for administering the program was given to the commissioner of agriculture, with a committee to advise the commissioner on the selection of farms. I served on that committee for five years.

Although the legislature supported the program, Governor Ella Grasso did not show much interest in preserving farms. It was generally perceived that she was more interested in the growth of industry. Nevertheless, the development rights of nine farms were negotiated promptly by Don Tuttle, who stayed attached to the Agriculture Department, and approved by George Wilber, Grasso's first commissioner. Leonard Krogh, her second commissioner, managed to avoid preserving any more farms during the balance of his term. Fortunately, when Governor O'Neill took office the purchase of development rights was resumed, and it has continued under Governor Weicker.

The program has been a success, limited only by the funds appropriated and by the steadily escalating cost of development rights. By the middle of 1992 136 farms totaling nearly 20,000 acres had been preserved at a cost to the state of $53.7 million. The existence of the program has also slowed the loss of other farms by demonstrating that farmers have an alternative to selling for development. Over a hundred of them have offered to sell their development rights in the future. I have been given considerable credit for my part in the establishment and progress of farmland preservation in the state. It is certainly one of the most useful projects I ever worked on and has always been for me a great source of pride and satisfaction.

When I helped initiate the farmland preservation program in 1974 it did not occur to me that I might want someday to sell my own development rights. A few years later that seemed to me the thing to do. I was approaching eighty, and I had no heirs trained or interested in carrying on the farm. After all I had put into it for nearly fifty years, I could not bear the thought of my land becoming a housing development. I resigned from the Preservation Advisory Committee and offered my development rights to the state.

My farm met the strict requirements of the law. It was under heavy development pressure; land was scarce and prices rising. There was a strong likelihood that one of the few good farms left in Fairfield County would be lost. The fertility of my soil, its capacity for producing food, ranked high. My farm market, selling a large part of what I grew direct to consumers, was a public asset. In 1983 my deal with the state was consummated, and the farm was restricted so that no structure may ever be built on it except a farm building. I was paid $6,000 an acre for my development rights. Since that time, with rising land prices, some rights purchases have cost much more, even in less-urbanized areas.

The event received wide publicity. I was surprised to find how many people told me they were pleased to have a permanently preserved farm in their part of the state. There were so few farms left in western Connecticut that the old Danbury Fair, once a genuine farm fair conducted by the Danbury Agricultural Society, had been abandoned. It was first taken over by a businessman who turned it into a vulgar money-making carnival, and later his heirs sold the site for a huge shopping mall.

Twenty-eight years of Apple Blossom Festivals, yearly visits of hundreds of schoolchildren, and the operation of a real farm market had built more goodwill for Blue Jay Orchards than I realized. People valued the very existence of a large open tract of land in what had become a suburban town, a place that reminded some people of their ancestral roots and of a way of life that was the everyday environment of their forebears. In addition to these sentimental and cultural factors, there was some economic benefit to the town. If the farm had become a housing development, Bethel would have had to build another school. Taxes on residences, unlike industrial and commercial property, do not pay for the schools and other services required.

When it became known that the land was available at agricultural value and was a practical investment for a farm enterprise, I was approached by several people who wanted to buy. In 1985 I sold everything except my house, a barn, and two acres to a businessman from Wilton, Connecticut, named Paul Patterson. I received about $2,000 an acre for my remaining equity in the restricted land, which was the approximate agricultural value, the amount a farmer might reasonably invest in land being farmed. Since I had been paid the difference between this agricultural value and what a developer might have paid, it was now possible for a new owner to continue operating Blue Jay on a sound economic base. This, of course, was the purpose of the program.

The sale of development rights does not include farm buildings or the land they stand on. The market and packinghouse, cider mill, four large cold-storage rooms, two poultry houses, two employee residences, and various garages and sheds were sold at market value, as were five tractors, three trucks, several sprayers, and a huge quantity of other equipment and supplies.

All this brought me more money than I ever expected to have. I paid off a substantial debt left from some bad crop years, I repaid Martha for money she had advanced many years earlier, and I did my duty by my old employees. Perhaps I should have sold the house then, but it had been my home for over fifty years, I had built parts of it myself, and we had raised a family in it. It was surrounded by thousands of trees which I had trained and nurtured, which had been a central part of my existence, and I hated to have them out of my sight. I had no illusions that any new owner would manage the farm exactly as I had, but I must say that I am not happy about how the trees and land are being cared for or about how well the purposes of the farmland preservation program are being served.

Having no farm to run after fifty years of taking care of all the details of a complicated business made a tremendous change in my life. Suddenly I had no more responsibility either for daily details or for seasonal planning. I had agreed to work closely with my successor, advising and instructing him and his employees, but by 1986 he apparently thought he had learned as much in a year as I had learned in fifty, and he stopped asking for my help.

I now had a lot more time and a little more money for environment programs. When the word got out that I had sold the farm I was offered many opportunities to make myself useful in organizations that I had long supported in a limited way, and soon I found that I had half a dozen new jobs and titles. Taking part in so many activities over so many years had given me a wide acquaintance among farmers, politicians, and newspeople, and that was very valuable in my new work.

There is a vast network of people working in the environment movement, volunteers like me and career professionals with formal training. A substantial majority of these are women. The organizations in this field divide between them the work of protecting natural resources, planning land-use, providing recreation, and controlling population growth. Lawyers play a major role in this. They write the laws and regulations we advocate and defend them in the courts. Yale and some other schools now have special programs in environmental law.

I was happy to take part in all of this. Some national associations like the Sierra Club and the Audubon Society were first identified with single issues but had become protectors of all natural resources, plants and animals, air and water. Others were strictly Connecticut enterprises. A state directory lists nearly 300 of these, of which 110 are municipal land trusts devoted to preserving local areas.

The staffs and volunteer members of these organizations conduct complex and far-reaching programs. They range from support of scientific research at the Agricultural Experiment Station to lobbying and publishing by the Land Conservation Coalition, which joins the voices of the whole environmental community in support of public projects and policy.

I testified before committees of the legislature, helped prepare publicity, and spoke at many meetings. One of these was an annual conference of the American Association for the Advancement of Science in Boston, where I discussed the problem of preserving farmland in the Northeast. When I was no longer farming, this was the chief outlet for my energy and experience.

For centuries people have used their control over the earth and its resources to develop ever more powerful and efficient technologies. These were the engines that drove civilization. Senator Al Gore, in his book *Earth in the Balance*, wrote: "As long as civilization as a whole continues to follow a pattern of thinking that encourages the domination and exploitation of the natural world for short-term gains, this juggernaut will continue to devastate the earth no matter what any of us does. . . . We must take bold and unequivocal action; we must make the rescue of the environment the central organizing principle for civilization."

This expresses, as well as anything I have read, the resolve that motivates those of us who call ourselves environmentalists. Some of this resolve grows directly out of people's experiences, some out of religious principles, some from simple concern for the welfare of fellow humans, a little out of enlightened self-interest, and in most of us there is a bit of healthy ego satisfaction that should not be denied. There is even, in the nineties, a need to be in style, but that no doubt will pass.

As I expected, I found among environmentalists, as I had among political radicals, a few whose devotion could only be called fanaticism, but there was not much of this. Perhaps the scale of our problems in dealing with nature is so overwhelming that there is little room left for the kind of absolute faith in an ideology that so often blinds political activists.

There was a time, however, when many farmers like me thought that some of the boosters of "organic" farming were fanatical in their belief that they alone were following practices beneficial to the land and to the consumer. They called their methods alternative agriculture, and they liked to think of themselves as a special cult, a group having an exclusive sacred ideology. They suggested that they were morally superior to farmers who were so crass as to try to produce the most food possible and to make a profit doing so.

The term "organic" may have seemed revolutionary, but farmers know that all farming was organic until late in the history of agriculture when scientists identified the chemical elements and learned which of them are needed for plant growth. These elements can be obtained from manure, certain plant tissues, and other natural sources, but chemical fertilizers are more economical. I once knew an otherwise educated man who believed that the chemical elements are not always the same, that, for instance, the phosphorus in certain rocks is different from the phosphorus obtained by a synthetic process. This of course is a physical and chemical impossibility.

In 1979 I attended a large assembly of northeastern farmers in New Jersey at which a conspicuous participant criticized in extreme terms both the methods and philosophy of conventional agriculture. One of his beliefs was that it is more admirable to have a small farm than a large one. He did not suggest that farmers have any responsibility for feeding people. He felt that only small hobby farmers like himself really care about the land and are able to obtain spiritual satisfaction from working it. The people at the meeting had come to discuss farm policy, economics, research, and technology. The cultural and spiritual returns from their lives and work were taken for granted. The self-absorbed advocate of "alternate" farming was unable to understand this.

It is not surprising that farmers are not enchanted by this kind of performance and that it delayed serious efforts by growers to try organic methods. Inevitably, however, the failure of standard practices to wipe out insects and plant diseases and the rising cost of chemicals and fertilizers have had their effect. A substantial number of commercial farmers have finally decided to consider organic practices and to test their economic feasibility.

Organic farmers oppose the use of chemicals either for fertilizer, for protecting plants against insects and diseases, or for limiting growth of weeds. There are biological controls for a few pests, but organic growers must accept a high percentage of defective fruits and vegetables. All this adds up to higher prices for produce, but as consumers learn about the effects of chemicals on the environment, some of them are showing a willingness to pay more for organically grown food and to accept fruits and vegetables with less than perfect complexions. These higher prices have led to some fraudulent use of the organic label; it is difficult to prove to what extent, if at all, organic principles have been observed by a grower.

A decade after the New Jersey conference the ideas of organic farming had made some headway on commercial farms. It had not yet been demonstrated that crops entirely free of insect and disease damage can be grown without chemicals, but changes in agriculture were reducing the effectiveness of the usual methods. The development of biological and genetic controls, offering hope for future solutions, proceeds slowly. Meanwhile the cost of farm chemicals escalates steadily.

Research scientists have introduced modifications in cultural practices called Integrated Pest Management, or IPM, which can reduce the use of chemicals, but its success depends on the ability of the grower to identify pests and to spray at precisely the right time. Many environmentalists concentrate their efforts on banning the use of all chemicals, without sufficient concern for how this would reduce the food supply. They also do not seem aware that many plants, to protect themselves against insect, fungus, and animal predators, produce natural toxic pesticides at far greater levels than the chemicals people apply.

Environment organizations, with all their programs and public support, have built an impressive, politically influential structure of scientific and legal talent. They would do better, in my opinion, to direct more of this power at increasing government and private expenditures for research in biology and genetics. Research could do much more to eliminate the use of chemicals than could agitation to ban them.

The U.S. Department of Agriculture (USDA), which should be leading the search for new ways of protecting plants, has until recently concentrated on trying to make old methods more efficient, thus encouraging the use of more chemicals and fertilizer. Critics suggest that its activities bring more benefit to manufacturers than to farmers. Even if it is accepted that its chief responsibility is to the farm industry and not to consumers, there remains the question of who benefits finally from its huge expenditures.

The USDA has tremendous research capacity, and the environmental community must increase its efforts to change how that capacity is used. The farm bill passed in 1990 by Congress suggests that even a bureaucracy as large as the USDA can change, or be changed. The law mandates, among other things, that the department expand the Low Input Sustainable Agriculture program for reducing the use of chemicals and increase expenditures for research on sound agronomic, economic, and environment programs. It also aims to reduce "pork barrel" funding, appropriations for dubious state and local agricultural projects that bring political benefits to politicians.

The fear that we are all being poisoned got its impetus from Rachel Carson's 1962 book *Silent Spring*, in which she showed that DDT and other chlorinated hydrocarbons could persist in the environment and the food chain. Farmers were by that time shifting to newer phosphate-based chemicals which were more effective against insect pests. Carson failed to mention that some of these new materials, while highly toxic when first applied, break down in the air and quickly become harmless to animals and humans. Such selectivity in choosing her facts led many informed people to question her conclusions and limited the value of her work, but on the whole her warnings were useful.

In the eighties public alarm was fed by the catastrophic leak of chemicals in Bhopal, India, and some politicians were exploiting this fear with demagogic pronouncements. I knew from my contacts with scientists that these dangers were being exaggerated, proving again the old saying that "exact knowledge is a great handicap to forcible statement." Some environmental groups, however, seemed glad to believe the worst.

The Natural Resources Defense Council (NRDC), which I had long supported because of its effective work on environmental issues, claimed that growers and government agencies were hiding the facts about the dangers of pesticides. As both a farmer and an environmentalist, I was asked in 1989 by Senator Christopher Dodd of Connecticut to testify at a Washington, D.C., hearing about the use of the chemical Alar on apples.

I found myself in the middle of this controversy, walking a chalk line between my emotional commitment to the agenda of my environmentalist friends and the objective reports of my associates in science. The star at the Dodd hearing was the actress Meryl Streep. Speaking for the NRDC, she said she feared that her children might contract cancer from eating apples. The photographers gave her their attention, but the reporters concentrated on the testimony of officials of the Environmental Protection Agency and the Food and Drug Administration. These scientists called the current fears exaggerated and explained government procedures that protect the public.

A healthy outcome of the hearing, and of the press reaction to the furor, was a widespread discussion of risks and risk assessment, emphasizing the hazards faced by people in their daily lives and the impossibility of attaining an entirely risk-free society. It was also demonstrated several years later, when ongoing research was completed, that Alar was much less toxic than had been claimed. By that time it was no longer being manufactured, and the apple growers whose business had been destroyed had either gone through bankruptcy or had been saved by crops on which no Alar was used.

This controversy about the use of a single farm chemical, which Senator Dodd thought merited the attention of his committee in 1989, raised questions of environmental policy which are, as I write, a major issue of the 1992 presidential campaign. The division on this question is as sharp as any I have seen in my time; surely no other decision will have as much effect on our future.

On one side we find those who believe that we must conserve the resources of the earth if life is to exist in the future, that we must reverse the trends begun by humans when they started to civilize themselves by exploiting other living organisms, both animal and plant, and abusing the soil and water on which we all depend for life. Protecting the environment is not just an aesthetic choice that we might like to embrace. It is a choice between life and a slow death for our race and for all the creatures that share the planet with us.

Opposing this belief are those who tell us that a sick economy can only be made healthy by selling our natural resources. We are advised to cut irreplaceable forests, drain valuable wetlands for real-estate development, graze public lands until they are deserts, strip-mine our mountains, divert our water to the cities, and allow industry to pollute air and water. These same people say we should not interfere with the growth of a population which already exceeds the ability of the earth to support it. They tell us that providing jobs now is more important than providing for the survival of our grandchildren.

Whatever voters may say in 1992, the struggle will go on. The stakes are so tremendous that no person of goodwill can doubt what choice we will finally make. Are we alarmed enough to make that choice now?

15 🍎 A Century of Change

I have absolutely no doubts about the importance to our future of the issues for which I work. I have tried to give all the time and money I could spare to the preservation of natural resources, the protection of wildlife, and the elimination of pollution and overpopulation. My long association with the Experiment Station has enabled me to support scientific research for backing-up such projects. These are important goals, and I have never questioned the need for attaining them. I do not take for granted, however, that the success of these programs will solve our basic social problems or that an improved environment can in itself meet all our social needs.

In the seventeenth and eighteenth centuries John Locke and other empirical philosophers assumed that human adaptability is practically unlimited, that man, with a history of some three million years of hunting and gathering and ten thousand years of agriculture, could adapt himself to an industrial and largely urban society in one to two hundred years. They assumed that man was born as a blank slate, bearing no marks of his history, and that society could draw on that slate a complete picture of the new, modern man.

The failures of that philosophy are more apparent every day. The early pressures of industrialism and exploitation have been somewhat modified by trade unionism and expanded social services, but we can see now that we have not adapted as easily to modern life as Locke and others expected. We see rising dissatisfaction with the workplace, loss of productivity, people struggling to escape the machine. What we call alienation increases. Crime exceeds in violence anything we have ever known. Widespread senseless vandalism threatens both urban and rural peace. Vulgar greed, and the corruption it breeds, overwhelms our economic structure. The integrity of our elected leaders is in question. As solutions to this profound dilemma we are offered Draconian law enforcement on one hand, more recourse to psychiatry and cults on the other.

It took us a long time to understand the effect of our life patterns on our bodies. We have finally learned to count the cost of neglecting our environment and are slowly cleaning up the air and water, improving nutrition, and expanding recreation facilities. We have a long way to go with these programs, but it seems to me that even a perfected environment will not by itself eliminate the conflict between the way we live and our biological inheritance.

We win victory after victory in the environmental wars, but the behavior problems of society do not go away. Has the crowding of people and the expansion of technology forced us too quickly into work patterns and social habits that deny our biological heritage? Does "quality of life" mean only a clean environment, a decent house, a steady job, an ample supply of goods, a pleasant place to play?

Can we add to our understanding of the physical needs of our planet a greater understanding of the social needs of man, an understanding of the effects of industrial society on behavioral health? Can we restore the ancient relation of man to nature, or must we ignore the frustrations of the hunter out of the woods, the fisher called from the sea, the farmer off the land, the builder bereft of tools? If we cannot, we may be saving the planet from destruction but permitting its inhabitants to destroy one another.

This is the unsolved problem we are leaving to future generations, the challenge for the twenty-first century. I would like to be here to see how we meet it.

I grew up in the twentieth century among people whose lives were severely narrowed by economic and social custom, whose biological heritage had largely been forgotten. They lacked what I call roots. As I matured I was determined not to repeat their pattern. I wanted, as does everyone, to be comfortable in my environment, to find satisfaction in my work, to enjoy and respect my neighbors. I thought for a while that I could continue indefinitely as both a book designer and a farmer, but I still had to decide where I would make my home, what kind of relations I would have with the people around me, how I should raise my children.

It seemed to me that the people I knew in Weston and Westport—artists, writers, actors, advertising geniuses—were as rootless as the businesspeople I grew up with. They were no more self-sufficient; they were equally dependent for their comfort and security on servants and artisans. They enjoyed the landscape, clean air, and access to Long Island Sound, but they were not part of any real community. What was missing was the interdependence of working together, having children in the schools, taking part in local government, sharing family histories.

I did not feel at home in such a society, but I did not at first realize that if I tried to live indefinitely with one foot in an urban industry and one in a small-town farm I could never put down the roots that I lacked, that I would be living a life as artificial as the one against which I had rebelled as a child.

I always believed, and was often told by friends, that I was by temperament an individualist, but my experience in the labor movement working with others for the general good and getting a glimpse of utopia showed me the limits of the independence I had always cherished.

Fortunately, although I did not at first realize it, farming in a small town was the best possible way to put down the roots I had never felt. People from the community became employees or suppliers of goods and services; thousands of them ate the food I grew. I became involved (sometimes entangled) in Bethel politics and town affairs, as my activities elsewhere had predicted. And last, there was the literal rooting in the soil of my trees and my fortunes.

I knew when I committed myself to farm life that I was finally giving up any opportunities I might have for wealth or worldly achievement. My vocation was not one that produced great movers and shakers. I always thought, idly, that it would be nice to be famous, but no choice that I ever made was actually aimed in that direction.

I was not obsessed by the need to put down roots; it was for long an unarticulated thought behind my decisions, but before I reached forty I was aware that having roots in a place was as important to me as the work I did there. It did not seem to me that everyone I knew felt this need; it was clearly the product of my origin and experiences.

I find it interesting to think about the relation of my friends to their social environment. Malcolm Cowley, born in Pittsburgh, was a literary critic and poet I had known since the thirties when he was a *New Republic* editor and a member of the Guild. He was also a friend of Sandy Calder; we celebrated their fortieth birthdays in 1938 at a famous party in the Calders' Roxbury house.

Malcolm lived in Sherman, near me, a part of the busy small-town life there. He edited a weekly paper, served on the zoning board and the land trust, and was for fifty years a part of Sherman life while writing his many books and even while going frequently to New York to the *New Republic* office. He could not have had deeper roots in Sherman if he had been born there and farmed there all his life. When he died a few years ago he was buried in the local churchyard. He was not in any way a religious man, but his body belonged to Sherman.

Arthur Miller, the playwright, is one of my few surviving contemporaries. He was born and raised in New York City. Since the forties he has had a house in Roxbury and hundreds of acres of land which he loves. He grows shade trees for a hobby, but I have always felt that he was a sort of permanent tourist in Litchfield County. He himself wrote in his autobiography, *Time Bends*, "I have lived more than half my life in the Connecticut countryside, all the time expecting to get some play or book finished so I can spend more time in the city."

Arthur's life was of course complicated by the fact that he could write his plays anywhere, but they needed urban stages and audiences to give them full life. I had other friends like him, mostly in Litchfield County, the most beautiful and least urbanized part of the state. They could work wherever there was a typewriter or an easel. They lived there to enjoy the landscape and the quiet, but publicity is essential to their careers, and some became what are called celebrities. Having public reputations sometimes stood between them and their communities; they could not tell whether their neighbors' interest was friendship or curiosity.

After fifty-seven years in Bethel I had to leave my own roots. I sold my house, and on my eighty-eighth birthday I went to live in

Experiment Station field day, Hamden, 1986

Hamden, a large Connecticut town on the edge of New Haven. Six years of seeing the farm abused was a factor in my moving, but so were the high cost of maintaining the house and my family's urging me to live where I could have easier access to medical facilities. I regretted leaving the big house in which my children grew up and which had remained the symbolic center of the family no matter where they were. Bethel and Danbury newspapers printed this farewell letter, along with stories and an editorial about my long involvement in local and state affairs.

To the Editor:

This is a letter of farewell to my neighbors and friends in Bethel and nearby towns. After 57 years here, I am going to live in Hamden at a place where I will have access to health care services if I need them. I will continue to spend most of my time working for the protection of land and other natural resources.

When I came here in 1934, at the age of 31, Bethel was a country town of 4,000 people. Since then it has doubled and then doubled again. There have been many changes, not all of them for the better.

We have been generous supporters of our elderly, and of recreation for everyone. I wish we were equally generous to our children and did more to help prepare them for an increasingly complex and competitive world. In a democracy, paying taxes for this is a privilege, not a burden. They provide the fuel that runs the engines of a caring society. There are some people who want us to forget that.

I have written a memoir to be published soon, an account of my experiences in many activities in Bethel and elsewhere. I have tried to be frank about people and events and I have not hidden my own sins of commission and omission.

I hope I will be remembered kindly. I know I have irritated some people, but the Bible says, "Woe unto you when all men shall speak well of you." I am not going very far away, but leaving the town that has been good to me for so long is not easy. I shall miss you all.

Robert Josephy

I compressed myself and my essential belongings into a well-equipped small apartment in a place called Whitney Center, where several of my friends from the Experiment Station have settled in retirement. After priding myself on my lifelong independence and self-sufficiency, I became a parasite, snug in a cocoon with most of my needs taken care of by others. New Haven, one of America's oldest cities, has a busy cultural life centered around Yale University. I have always had friends there, and I now live only five minutes from the station.

Whitney Center, a huge six-story building, could not be more different from the farm. I have always had a variety of friends in many places but few nearby. Now, after living alone for years and seeing many old friends die, I have over two hundred new neighbors living only a few feet away. I wondered how I would be able to communicate with them all, but this has not proved to be difficult. I have found more compatible people than I expected and have made many new friends.

As in all so-called retirement communities, 80 percent of the people in Whitney Center are women. I do not find that daunting. I find that I am losing my old habit of looking at women as sex objects. Any satisfaction I gain, however, in finding that my real responses are becoming more consistent with my theoretical feminist beliefs is tempered by realizing that this may be because of my loss of sexual competence. Happily, I can still find pleasure in looking at pretty young waitresses in the center's dining hall.

The people in this place have not only retired from their jobs but have left their families and communities. In the past most elderly people stayed with their families; now they end up in artificial environments like this one. In many cases their narrowing experiences concentrate their attention on food and weather and such matters, but many are sophisticated persons who have not lost their broad interests. To serve them the center has a full-time organizer of recreational and cultural events, including trips to plays, concerts, and museums.

Differing from my life in Bethel, where I had put down deep roots so long ago, I have not become involved in the town of Hamden. Running an enterprise that was part of the life of Bethel was as important to me as growing my crops. I could not do that again if I tried. I am now approaching ninety, and my sole function here is to be a resident.

My health is better than I have any right to expect; the details of my few afflictions would not make interesting reading. I have had short periods of intense pain while working on this manuscript, and it sometimes seems as if that has been a stimulus to my imagination. Thanks to inherited genes, no tobacco, and a good drink of whiskey every evening, I am still able to drive to meetings around Connecticut and serve on the boards of half a dozen environment and research organizations, but I know I am slowing up. Often I catch people deferring to my age; almost always now they greet me by saying in a surprised tone, "You *are* looking very well."

I find that many people think that to survive is in itself an accomplishment, as if the free ride through time that one's ancestors' genes have given one is more than a happy accident. Still, if longevity keeps the brain clicking and not simply the heart pumping, there are uses for accumulated experience, and people seem to value that. The trick is to avoid trading on one's age, to avoid agreeing that wisdom always comes with it, and to avoid accepting at face value every expression of goodwill.

Most of my activity is still focused on the protection of Connecticut's land and water resources. Even in this small busy state we are not insulated from larger problems of overpopulation, atmospheric change, and the extinction of plant and animal species. Environmental groups, whatever their original special fields, are now addressing these broad questions. Public support grows steadily, but we still have a long way to go. A recent study found that the average American family contributes thirty-eight times as much to religion as to the environment, five times as much to education, and twice as much to the arts.

This book has not turned out to be, as I expected, a straightforward chronology of my taking part in many activities both as advocate and participant, telling where I had been, what I had done, who I had known. Little did I expect that writing it would be like living my life over again, examining myself as I had hardly done from day-to-day.

I have always liked to think of myself as a potential writer. I started contributing to school publications at an early age and to the *Flushing Journal* when I was fourteen. I have frequently written essays and criticism on subjects that have occupied me and have enjoyed sending letters, mostly controversial, to newspapers. None of this has included much about my innermost feelings or my reactions to people.

Although in 1920 I wanted a job that could lead to a writing career, I was easily diverted by circumstance to the work of transmitting other writers' thoughts to readers. As I matured, it turned out that my temperament was not well suited to a life of study and contemplation, and I learned that there were other ways to use my imagination. It was only after a lifetime of intense activity, dealing with ideas, enterprises, and people, that the project for this book surfaced. I was not prepared with a set of diaries or journals; my files only had some letters and a lot of newspaper clippings. Fortunately, I found in my memory a store of facts and impressions that I did not know was there.

Searching for a logical pattern in my life has been an absorbing experience. Some people can examine their lives as they live them, but that was not my way. Whether being so busy really left me little time for thought or was an unconscious excuse for not facing the significance of my actions or their effect on others, I cannot say.

I was aware of how my tastes and prejudices were formed by my background and early experiences, but this understanding did not yield any fixed plan for my life. I always felt free to investigate new possibilities and changes of direction. I thought I would try to become a writer, but working for a publisher led me to designing and fabricating books. My fascination with how things are made should have warned me which way I would go. Later I should not have been surprised to find in farming a sphere for exercising my sense of order and for creating the sort of world I wanted to live in. I believe that this yearning for order, more than any other aspect of my temperament, drove me to oppose economic disorder and the injustices that went with it. I found in labor organization, in politics, and in efforts to protect the physical world the same challenges I had found in trying to create on paper an orderly presentation of a writer's ideas and words.

As I again become involved in a publishing project, this time as an author, it is interesting to see how printing methods have changed in half a century and to assess at this distance the work I did as a designer of books and what influence I had.

New inventions in printing technology have brought about a revolution comparable to the invention of movable metal type in the fifteenth century, but it is still the function of the printer to fabricate a bridge between the minds of the writer and the reader. Printers are as constrained as ever by having limited control over the quality of materials and workmanship, and of course no control over the words that they are asked to arrange with taste and logic.

The types devised in the fifteenth century were intended to look like books written or lettered by hand, but the design of the alphabet still established the style of the printed book. Type was made by carving a letter onto the head of a metal punch, striking the punch into softer metal to make a matrix, and using the matrix as a mold for casting single letters. These would then be composed into a page, inked, and impressed upon paper. The type designer's hand and personality are conveyed through this process as in few other works of craftsmanship.

Today the text of a book is written on a computer or word processor. It is stored on a disk, corrected as necessary, and transferred photographically to a lithographic printing plate. The image is then inked and transferred again to a rubber-covered roller which deposits it on a sheet or roll of paper.

Even from this very short description it can be seen how letters that have gone through this process would look quite different on the page from those printed from metal type. Some alphabets have been designed to fit this new technology, and many old ones have been modified for it. Discipline and taste are still needed; the typographer is still using type and paper to convey information and feelings.

The design problems offered by this new technology were to some extent foreseen by artists in the Bauhaus in the twenties and by a few others in Europe. Their new perceptions grew out of new inventions, new ways of manufacturing goods and building structures, that were evident before the camera revolutionized printing. Their way of seeing things was expressed in a style, a set of design principles, that came to be called modernism.

I saw that these principles could help solve typographic problems. The most elementary of the ideas they conveyed was that it was not radical but only logical for a typographic layout to be asymmetrical, if that departure from convention gave it order, grace, and legibility. That simple idea freed typography from the conformity of having each line of type centered on the page and from other rigid customs. It introduced to printing the flexibility from which design in many other fields has benefited.

These ideas were reflected in my work and encouraged my efforts to influence the work of my contemporaries. Very little specific criticism was written about the design of books when I was producing a great many of them. As I remember it, there were efforts to encourage designers whose intentions were good but very little appraisal of their accomplishments. *Publishers Weekly*, whose editor, Fred Melcher, had a genuine missionary zeal for promoting good bookmaking, gave substantial space to designers but seldom discussed in detail the taste or technical competence they showed.

I know of only two serious critiques of my own work. Percy Seitlin in 1941 called it clean, honest, and straightforward. Charles Farrell, in a review I quoted in chapter 5, called it simple, clean-cut and tasteful, wholly free from idiosyncrasy and affectation. Both these critics seem to say that I succeeded in what I was trying to do. They also suggest that I avoided attempts at self-expression, the injection of the designer's ego which vulgarizes so much of contemporary typography and often obscures the clear expression of a writer's meaning.

I may have tried to produce too many books, and perhaps gave insufficient time and thought to some of them. Looking at my books now, I see some that show this, but there are many that I am still proud of. I am encouraged to recall how many publishers, large and small, hired me to design for them and what a great variety of books I had a chance to work on.

I did accomplish certain things. I pioneered in establishing the free-lance designer as a factor in the book industry. I helped to prove that good work could be done in large book-manufacturing plants and that mass production was respectable. I demonstrated that designers need not live in ivory towers, that their work could relate to their social principles and to activity in several fields of endeavor.

Why did I give up a career that was satisfying and reasonably lucrative? I did not decide arbitrarily at any point that I was finished. I guess I thought that I might work at both typography and agriculture forever. The decision was made day-to-day: What shall I do today? What is more urgent? What is more interesting? As the farm grew in size and I learned more about farming, I became increasingly excited about the possibilities. There was more to learn than I had anticipated, more new challenges to my abilities and imagination, and many interesting things to do off the farm that were related to the science and business of agriculture.

I have never to this day stopped looking for possibilities in a new piece of copy to be designed and printed. I still await eagerly the sight of the first proofs, but for me agriculture became a constantly widening field, and typography no longer was.

What was there in my education that prepared me for the work I did as an adult? Like all secondary schools, BMI liked to boast about how many of its graduates were accepted by colleges, but little time was given to discussing why a boy should attend one. Trained guidance counselors did not exist. The teachers could have shared their wisdom, but it was left to parents to shape their sons' futures.

I was under no pressure from my family to continue my studies; for the kind of career they envisioned I would not need that. Their generation of comfortable businesspeople, whatever their family histories, had little respect for learning for its own sake. Immigrants coming from western Europe in the mid-nineteenth century, like my German grandfather, were not fleeing oppression but simply seeking economic opportunity. They spawned more merchants and lawyers than academics.

The generation that followed them to America came largely from eastern Europe and were escaping severe economic, political, and religious oppression. They had powerful motivations to see that their children became scientists, teachers, artists, philosophers. This pattern was seen again late in the twentieth century among immigrants from Asia.

What I wanted most in 1920 was independence. I wanted a job, and I thought I could get an education while I worked. If I had not been so eager to be on my own and had spent the next four years in college I would have been exposed to ideas and influences different from those in the job I found, but perhaps not any more valuable. On the other hand, before getting deeply involved in work I might have learned more about myself, my needs, and my aptitudes.

I have always liked to quote the mathematician and philosopher Alfred North Whitehead who said, "The educated man is the self-educated man." I received my education from the people I knew, from the history and the problems of the projects in which I took part, from the information I had to acquire to meet my goals. I assume that is the sort of education Whitehead was talking about. I know I was aided by a healthy curiosity and an unwillingness to accept the world as it was presented to me by others.

I have occasionally thought of architecture as a career I should have tried if I had gone to college. It might have offered more scope for my imagination than did typography. That was an obvious idea, the problems of the architect and the typographer are very much alike. I might, however, have been frustrated by the small number of projects that an architect can manage in a lifetime and the magnitude of any failure. The opportunity I had to produce a great number of books was some insurance against that kind of disappointment.

From working in agriculture and the environment movement I have acquired a modest layman's knowledge of the natural sciences. My association with the scientists and their research work at the Experiment Station has of course encouraged this. I think that scientific investigation is a career to which my temperament and way of thinking might have suited me. I have no illusions, however, that I might, starting from an interest in literature and printing, have ended up as a scientist.

The biggest gap in my education comes from my failure to spend enough time reading. I was always aware of this, but I could never resist filling my time with too many other things that demanded immediate attention. There is practically no kind of book that does not give me pleasure or stimulation, but I care least about reading novels. Perhaps in fiction, as in life, I tend to avoid involving my emotions. This may explain my limited interest in music. I have attended enough concerts and recitals to know what I was missing, but I have to conclude that, while I admire the structure of a composition, I do not care enough about hearing it played to give much time to musical performances.

While it is true that I do not look for emotional stimulation in literature or music, I certainly do have strong feelings about nature, art, social questions, and personal relations. I have always enjoyed the company of women and have spent a great deal of time with them, probably more than the average man. I have worked with them in the labor and environment movements, in publishing, and in politics. I have also sought their companionship for pleasure, comfort, and intellectual stimulation. Sometimes my interest has been frivolous, but many of my longest and most rewarding friendships began as romantic episodes.

I have known great passion, but the occasions are rare. My responses were sometimes more intense than my companion's, sometimes less so. I guess those are the stones that are said to lie in the path of true love. I am generally thought to be a serious and diligent person, and I have never felt any conflict between my public and private lives, but I occasionally wonder whether the one seems to some people inconsistent with the other.

I like to think of myself as supporting feminist ideas. I was slow in realizing how women have been exploited; in fact, I cannot be sure that they have never been exploited by me. I certainly feel strongly now that constraints on women's rights, independence, and opportunities will have to be removed before we can attain a healthy society or a prosperous one.

My late enlightenment may explain why I have not been a very satisfactory husband. Perhaps I should not have remarried after the failure of my first attempt, but I certainly did not enjoy the half-life of a single man that I lived during the nine years between my two marriages. On the other hand, I have always taken perverse pleasure in recalling what Babe LaPine, my barber for many years, said to me after the death of his wife, "I loved her, Bob, just as if we had never been married."

I have faced several major choices in my life, and I always tried to keep myself free to make them. I often think of my lawyer and longtime close friend, David Chipman. He is a generation younger, but we share strong feelings about the same questions and have supported one another in many difficult situations. Our histories differ, however. I have usually managed to be free to make choices, but Dave's commitment to a demanding law practice and the maze of personal obligations in which he always seems to live constantly frustrate, or at best limit, his freedom of action.

As for me, I was fortunate in not feeling committed to any one vocation or, until my life was fixed in agriculture, to any one place. I was also never limited by economic considerations, as I would have been if I was determined to get rich, and I never felt bound by what people call tradition.

George Howe, an architect, once said, "Tradition is a transmitted habit of behavior which relieves men of making thoughtful decisions at every step. Without it life would be a succession of intolerable hesitations. With it we are condemned to an almost insuperable inertia."

I found that it was easy to make a dent in the brittle body of tradition, armed with an optimistic temperament and an unwillingness to accept the status quo. It is popular to say that if something ain't broke, don't fix it. If you believe, however, that there are usually several stages between unbroken and broke, you can see many opportunities to do something useful.

It surprised me to find how few people, how little power, how modest a resolve, it takes to bring about change. That is of course not always true. The social changes we have seen in the twentieth century required tremendous effort, but many small changes that add up to make big ones are within the capacity of anyone who has the courage to work for them.

I was born near enough to the end of the nineteenth century to see as a child the remnants of Victorian ideas and attitudes. People of goodwill, like my family, felt an obligation to care about the poor and the disabled. The practice of charity, largely based on organized religion, has developed in the twentieth century into a sophisticated philanthropy, directed at promoting social change as well as at alleviating suffering. This has sometimes been called an exercise in atonement, an attempt at altering the image of the exploiter and robber baron. Whatever the motives, however, private institutions have often shown the way to government in meeting social needs, especially in education, health, civil rights, racial tolerance, and the environment.

Changes in technology may encounter the resistance of skeptics, but the profit in adopting them usually ensures their acceptance. In my lifetime I have seen advances in transportation and communication that have at the same time stretched and shrunk the planet. I have seen us unlock the atom, escape the earth's gravity, extend the reach of our brains with the computer, and start on the probably endless road of genetic engineering.

We have been at war through most of the century. An unforeseen consequence of our technical triumphs is that we can no longer indulge safely in that pleasure. The development of nuclear weapons has made decisive victory impossible and narrowed the difference between war and suicide. Science has given us a power that we do not dare use, and the majority of scientists do not now justify our having used it in 1945.

Scientists do not usually want their work subjected to moral judgment. As a layman, observer, and supporter of scientists I am under no such constraints and am quite willing to affirm that the scientific work I have seen has been of great benefit to humanity. I am willing to go further and claim that most of my own personal activities have had positive value. Choosing them was never difficult; my temperament and my experiences left me few alternatives.

I had to decide, of course, where I could be most useful. I have strong feelings about the rights and opportunities of women and racial minorities. I believe that the future of our democracy will depend on whether these groups gain their rightful place in society and are enabled to contribute their talents and energies. It seemed to me, however, that my experience and aptitude could be best applied to the problems of feeding people and protecting their environment, and that is where I have worked during the last half of my life.

It is not fitting for me to judge myself, but I have to believe that my sins of omission and commission have largely been offset by the time and thought I have given to projects which brought me no material gain. These efforts earned me praise and a reputation for self-sacrifice, but I always knew that I was getting private satisfaction which more than repaid me. I suspect that I might not have been so devoted to these seemingly selfless endeavors if I were not receiving such returns. Many other useful citizens will admit to getting this kind of payoff. In fact, I am suspicious of those who are willing to let it be said that their good works are inspired entirely by nobility of character.

This account of my life and concerns is unfinished. As I write the last pages the American people are engaged in deciding the future direction of our country. This will be determined not only by a national administration but by the Congress and the state governments we choose. Like many others, I have hopes that the women who are moving into positions of responsibility will make a difference. I have lived long enough to know that no election can bring about the end of the world, but the success of many of the things I have worked for hangs in the balance this year.

I lived through the Great Depression, and I saw what the American people, given the right kind of leadership, can do to change the course of history. Always an optimist, I am confident that they are ready to do it again.

Before you read this book, you and I will know.